The Garbage Bag Kids

Virginia Jeffers

The true story of one family's thirty-year journey through the maze of the foster care system

Library of Congress Cataloging-in-Publication Data

Jeffers, Virginia

The Garbage Bag Kids: one family's thirty- year journey through the maze of the foster care system.

Registration TXu-1-056-810

Effective Date of Registration 6-19-02

ISBN: 1502826011
ISBN 13: 9781502826015

Table of Contents

Acknowledgments

I appreciate and thank my husband, Jay, for his continuing love and support and the shared belief that every child deserves a happy childhood. Thank you for sacrificing of yourself to provide all the wonderful experiences for our family and the children who came into our home...experiences that make life worth living.

I thank my children, Brent and Janelle, for their unselfish sharing of their parents, their possessions, and their love with children less fortunate than themselves. I thank Janelle also for her continued help with the care of the foster children currently in our home. Thanks to Brent for designing the cover for this book.

A special thanks to my sister, Shirley Hoff, who, as an R.N. has been an invaluable medical resource through the years. Her advice and expertise when children's ailments, or tempers arose has been a wonderful blessing. She has been an "ear" to listen to my concerns and hopes and dreams for the special children placed in our care.
We shared the wonderful bond that only "sisters" share.

Thanks to the wonderful caseworkers we have known throughout the past 30 years. We could not have taken in these special "chosen" children if it were not for their support and encouragement.

Thanks also to Koinonia Foster Homes, and especially Miriam Golden for her vision to establish faith based foster Homes, and her continued dreams for her "chosen" children.

Thank you to all of the wonderful special education teachers, whose education, experience, and devotion, continue to help special needs children succeed to the best of their ability.

Thank you to all of the wonderful children who have crossed our doorstep. Thank you for your sweet smiles, all those hugs, your childlike faith, and your strength and determination. Your sweet daily prayers are a treasure we will keep in our hearts for eternity.

Lastly, but certainly not least, thank you to all of our dear friends and family, who, throughout the years, have welcomed, accepted, and loved the precious "chosen" children who have come to be a part of our family.

Prologue

At this time in the exercise, I feel large tears welling up within my eyes. I am growing short of breath. There is this big knot in the pit of my stomach. I cannot believe it... this is just a role play exercise... I am at a foster parents seminar .... The reality of what I'm feeling through acting out this scenario is so overwhelming I find myself beginning to weep. How could this happen to a little child? It is beyond comprehension to think I cannot return to my home. I will not be allowed to speak to my brother, my sister, or my school friends. How frightening for a child to be taken by strangers, and placed in a house with strangers, strange food, strange bed, unfamiliar surroundings. Even as I write this, my emotions begin to well up inside me.... This is just not right. This is too frightening an experience for anyone to endure, least of all a child. I never gave much credence to role-playing, but for some reason this time, this exercise, placing myself in the role of a 7-year-old girl, who has just been taken from her home and placed in a foster home, has hit home...and it is too painful to imagine.

But this is reality. It happens every day. Children taken from all that is familiar to them, placed in unfamiliar surroundings, with total strangers, and they must face it on their own.

How and where did our journey into the immense web of the foster system take place?

Before we begin our journey, let us consider some statistics illustrating major trends and issues in the child welfare system. All data are for the period ending Sept. 30, 2012, and are taken from: *Adoption and Foster Care Analysis and Reporting System (AFCARS)*

Children and youth at risk

- 903,000 children and youth were confirmed victims of abuse and neglect in the United States.

Children and youth in care

- 400,000 children and youth are in foster care on any given day in the United States.
- 35% all children in foster care are over the age of 10.

Length of stay in care for children and youth

- 46 percent are placed in the child welfare system for less than one year.
- 23 percent remain in the system for more than three years.
- 53 percent (or about 175,000 children) have reunification with their birth families as their case goal.

Caregivers

- 185,257 (47 percent) of the children in foster care live with licensed foster parents.
- 112,000 (28 percent) live with a relative.
- 60,000 (18 percent) are in a group home or institution.
- 20,289 (4 percent) are in pre-adoptive homes.
- 16,665 (3 percent) are in a trial home visit.
- 4,000 (1 percent) are runaways.
- 4,070 (1 percent are in supervised independent living.
- There were 155,355 licensed family (non-relative) foster homes and 18,439 kinship homes licensed as foster homes in the United States in 2000.

Kinship care (relatives or tribal members as caregivers)

- 109,000 or 24 percent of youth in foster care are placed with licensed foster parents who are also kin.
- In 2010, more than 2.9 million grandparents were the primary adults responsible for their grandchildren.

Siblings in care

- Note: National statistics are not available, and state data are limited. Estimates are over half of children in foster care have siblings who are also in care.

- For example: In January 2003, 69 percent of children in the California child welfare system had at least one sibling out-of-home care.
- In 1998 in the New York child welfare system, 64 percent of children had at least one sibling in out-of-home care.

Racial/ethnic group representation
- There are no differences based on race in the incidence of abuse and neglect of children and youth.
- African-American children and children of two or more races are four times more likely than Caucasian children to be placed in out-of-home care.
- Children of color are less likely to be reunified with their birth families.
- Children of color experience a higher number of placements.
- American Indian and Alaska Native children are three times more likely than Caucasian children to be placed in out-of-home care.

Why Children are in Foster Care –Excerpted from an October 1995 Newsletter of the Child Welfare League of America, Foster Care, F.Y.I. Posted: 7/97

Of the children who entered care in 1995:
*50% were for protective service reasons: 21% because of parental condition or absence (illness, death, handicap or financial hardship), 11% because of child's commitment status or delinquent offenses, 2% because of child's disability or handicap, 1% because of relinquishment of parental rights, 13% for other state-defined reasons (including a parent/child relationship or family interaction problem, an adoption plan or subsidized adoption, de-institutionalization, and unwed motherhood).

Alcohol and drug abuse are factors in the placement of more than 75% of the children who are entering care. Children who lose their parents to AIDS is another group in need of foster care. In addition, increasing numbers of children who are HIV infected are in foster care.

Many of the children coming into care today are medically fragile and/or physically handicapped. Between 1984 and 1990 there was a 12% increase in the number of children who entered foster care because of their own handicap or disability.

Children in foster care are three to six times more likely than children not in care to have emotional, behavioral and developmental problems including conduct disorders, depression, difficulties in school, and impaired social relationships. Some conservative estimates are about 30% of the children in care have marked or severe emotional problems. According to a GAO (1995) study, 58% of young children in foster care had serious health problems; 62% had been subject to prenatal drug exposure, placing them at significant risk for numerous health problems. The educational needs of children in care can be substantial. Various studies have indicated children and young people in foster care tend to have limited education and job skills; perform more poorly educationally than children who are not in foster care, lag behind in their education by at least one year, and have lower educational attainment than the general population.

Our story.
It all began in 1964 when my husband, Jay and I moved to Portland, Oregon with high hopes and dreams of being part owners in an optical coating business. With our youthful exuberance, Jay was just twenty-four and I was twenty, we were going into business with a friend. We were very young and naïve, but the opportunity seemed so perfect. With our little bundle of joy, fourteen months old Brent, safely tucked in his makeshift car bed, which Jay constructed from a wooden orange crate, and I had lined it with his favorite teddy bear quilt, we packed up our Volkswagen bug and made our journey northward. I can still see my father standing there with tears in his eyes, waving good-bye as he watched us drive away. We were a young couple off on a new adventure. There was no way we could have known the path this adventure would take....and how it would eventually lead us to the greatest adventure of all, the care and nurturing of severely neglected, abused and abandoned children.

Jay, my husband, was, and is, the love of my life. We were high school sweethearts, meeting in high school when I was just fourteen, a freshman and he was nearly nineteen and a senior. We dated for four years, and our courtship survived his eighteen-month tour of duty in the navy, the death of my mother when I was just seventeen, and the re-marriage of my father just six months later. We married when I was just eighteen and he was twenty-two. I have always considered it a blessing knowing the one thing I will never have to endure, as so many others have, is the loss of my very first true love and the pain of wondering what might have been. Through fifty years of marriage we have been, and still are, each other's greatest fan, best friend, lover and confidant. We could not ask for more.

After settling in Portland we worked long and hard for two years and the coating business was successful; however, our business savvy was not. Once the business began turning a profit, our business partner decided he did not want to share the profits. He had very cleverly drawn up the business partnership so that he was able to vote us out of the company and he took it all for himself. We had trusted him because he was a friend. It is of some consolation that when the customers we had serviced learned of his misdeeds they dropped him and the business was forced to close within a year. As disappointing as this was, we always knew God would work things out for us, He always had and He always would. In the meantime, Jay found another job working for United Medical Labs in Portland. The company very generously paid for his education to obtain his B.S. degree in Medical Technology and he began work as a Medical Technologist. Believe me, this was much less stressful than running the optical coating business had been.

Although on a very limited and meager budget, I was able to stay at home and take care of our precious baby boy, who was our total delight. Brent has always been a very happy boy, easy to smile, laugh, very bright and quick to learn. He brought us such happiness that soon we began thinking of having a second child. We discussed this with our physician, and were quite discouraged when he told us that, due to my RH-negative blood, and the fact that I had built up antibodies while carrying Brent, he did not recommend our having a second child for a couple more years. With our limited income, adoption was out of the question. The caseworker we had contacted regarding possible adoption suggested we might be interested in foster care. She indicated a real need for families to foster children in their homes. In 1964 the State laws regarding foster care required there be a stay at home parent. Since I had made the decision to be home with Brent, this would work out quite well for us. What the caseworker failed to tell us was, although you must care for the children as you would your own, you were not to love them to the extent that you could not give them up when the courts decided it was time for them to be returned to their biological parents, or placed for adoption. We would learn this later at the expense of a broken heart. We carefully considered the responsibilities of becoming foster parents and after completing mountains of paperwork, undergoing intensive background checks, thorough examinations of our home and even physical examinations, we were at last licensed to be foster parents with Multnomah County in Portland, Oregon.

In 1964 there was no orientation or training provided to prospective foster parents. There were no seminars on dealing with separation, grief, or emotional problems stemming from severe abuse, neglect and sexual molestation. Foster parents were not provided with any information regarding the history of the foster child to be placed in their care as this was considered "confidential." In short, we were ill prepared for what was to come.

I am pleased to report, although still a long way from perfect, the system has improved within the last three decades. Foster parents are now considered an integral part of the child's emotional healing. They are provided with history and background for each child. There are psychologists, psychiatrists and counseling for families to assure that optimal care be provided to each child. There are new laws and provisions protecting the rights of foster children and foster parents alike. We have come a long way to improve the foster care system. Social Services now contracts with private agencies to provide a major portion of foster care. These agencies have more reasonable work-loads, adequate staffing and available resources to ensure improved care of children within the foster care system. New requirements include long range planning for each child to ensure no child will become "lost in the system." However, we were not so fortunate when we began our journey into foster care in 1964.

Lynden

"Hi everybody, I'm home," announced the cheerful voice of the awkward, somewhere between boyhood and manhood fourteen-year-old. He was often embarrassed these days about his inability to control the squeaking in his voice which was changing. This accompanied with the red protrusions that would appear on his nose, chin and other conspicuous places were very disconcerting to the boy. It seemed at this stage of his life he was all legs and feet, and was somehow trying to grow into his body.

It was exciting the day the phone call finally came from the Multnomah County Social Services Caseworker. "Mrs. Jeffers, this is Ms. Randall, from Social Services. Your name has been given to me as a potential foster home placement for a child that I have who needs a home." "Oh, yes", I replied, trying to conceal the excitement I felt as we had been eagerly awaiting the opportunity to accept a child into our home. "Well," said Ms. Randall, "This child is not exactly what your application indicates you prefer, a child from two to four years of age, but let me tell you about this boy." Our little Brent was just barely two years old so we thought having a two to three year old foster child as a playmate for him would be preferable. However, that was not to be the case at this time.

Ms. Randall continued, "Lynden is a fourteen-year-old boy who is currently in foster care. His foster parents are requesting that he be moved at this time." I was to learn later in Lynden's previous foster home the family's biological son was feeling jealous and in competition with Lynden and had asked his father to have Lynden moved. This is

1

not an uncommon occurrence. Foster children are quite often moved from home to home, due to no fault of their own. Foster children may not get along with the family's biological children. The foster child may not survive the "honeymoon" period. Many children will "test" the new parents just to see "will you love me if I misbehave," and if foster parents are not aware of these testings they may become discouraged and give up on the child. This, of course, just re-enforces the child's belief that no one wants him, and he is not worthy of love, a home or family.

Some foster parents go into parenting with the idea that "love covers all." If I can just love this child enough, he will come around." This is not always the case. Many times love is not enough. Children need discipline, structure, security, and permanence in their lives. These children have not had the benefit of love that disciplines, or security, and they can neither give nor receive love as they cannot give or receive what they have never experienced.

The disappointment must have been evident in my reply "Oh, we really want a much younger child," but Ms. Randall did not miss a beat, she just went right on, "Oh, I know, Mrs. Jeffers, if you would just meet Lynden you would see what a nice young man he is." As we were quite eager to begin our role as foster parents, I agreed to meet Lynden the next afternoon.

He stood there rather awkwardly, staring down at the ground, a tall, 5 ft. 11 inch, lanky boy with dirty blonde hair. I reached out my hand and said, "Hi, Lynden, my name is Virginia, and I'm so pleased to meet you." He looked up at me and he had the most beautiful blue eyes and pleasant smile. He nervously shook my hand… "Uh, I'm pleased to meet you, too," He replied. Something inside of me, said, "This is a very nice, shy boy, who is in need of a home." But were we prepared to take this boy, this total stranger, a teenager into our home? We had a short conversation, said good bye and the caseworker and I agreed to talk the next day. She called me early the next morning, and following several more phone calls and one more visit, we agreed to have Lynden come to live with us.

He showed up on our doorstep with two large black garbage bags, which contained all of his possessions. The garbage bags held several sets of ill-fitting clothes, shoes that were too small for his feet, holey socks, a few books, tattered photographs and school items. This familiar scene was to be repeated many times over the next thirty years... kids and garbage bags....on our doorstep.

Most of us cannot imagine what it must be like for a child to be placed in the position of having to "interview" for placement in a foster home. Worst still, many foster children have the idea that foster homes are people just taking in children "for the money." They believe the foster parents do not really care about them. In some cases, unfortunately they have been right. These are quite often children who have been "in the system" for years, acted out, rebelled against mistreatment in a foster home, and then were shifted from home to home. This continues until the child is eighteen and then often he becomes a ward of the juvenile justice system.

It was not until years later, through a role-playing exercise at a seminar for foster parents I really came to appreciate the traumatic events that occur when a child is placed in foster care. At the seminar I was asked to assume the role of a six to seven year old child living at home. All at once there comes a knock at the door. When I answer the door there is someone from the police department accompanied by a social worker. I am told to gather up my belongings and, because I have no suitcase, the social worker hands me a large black garbage bag. I must gather up all of my clothes, toys, etc. and leave immediately with the social worker and policeman. I am then driven across town to the home of total strangers. At this point I am asked by the seminar director to imagine what I am feeling as the social worker introduces me to the woman of the house, who smiles sincerely, and takes me into her home. The woman says that I may call her Donna, and she gives me a tour of the house. She shows me to a room and tells me this will now be my room. At this point, I become terrified and begin to cry. I ask to call my brother and she tells me that this is not allowed. Once I get my garbage bag unpacked, the woman has provided me with two drawers of a dresser and a section of the closet to store my things. She then calls me to dinner. I am immediately admonished for failing to wash my hands and then escorted to the dinner table. At the table sit two adults I do not know, and two children who are whispering and giggling as they size up the newcomer to the table. I am not sure what to do at this point. The food does not smell like anything I am familiar with, and I do not know what to do with the various dishes on the table.

The seminar instructor asks us to jot down our feelings as after dinner we are directed to the bathroom where we are to bathe, in the presence or strangers, and then we are provided with pajamas and tucked into bed. At this time in the exercise, I could feel large tears welling up within my eyes. I am actually growing short of breath. I could not believe it... this is just an exercise... I am at a seminar.... Yet the reality of what I would be feeling were this scenario to actually happen to me is so strong I find myself beginning to weep. How could this happen to a little child? How horrible would it be to know I could not return to my home? I would not be able to speak to my brother, my sister, or my school friends. How overwhelming for a little child to be taken by strangers, and placed with strangers. Even as I write this, my emotions begin to stir.... This is not right. This is too frightening an experience for any one to have to endure, least of all, a child.

But it is reality. It happens every day. Little children taken from all that is familiar to them and placed in unfamiliar surroundings, with total strangers, and they must face it on their own.

One thing we were not prepared for was the lack of privacy that now existed in our home. Privacy was something we had always taken for granted. With a fourteen-year-old stranger now living in our house, the lack of privacy became quickly obvious, especially to me. No longer could I make a mad dash for the bedroom from the bathroom shower... nor could I run to answer the phone half dressed. With just a toddler this had not yet become an issue, but with a teenager in the house it very quickly became apparent never again would I have the freedom and privacy I had once enjoyed.

Also, Jay and I had to be very careful regarding the intimate areas of our life. We had always enjoyed the spontaneity and pleasure of our lovemaking. If we were listening to romantic music, or watching a love story on television in the living room, and the desire arose, we would make love right there on the spot. From here on out our lovemaking would either take place strictly in the bedroom, or in the afternoon when Lynden was still at school.

Now these may seem like trivial things, and I did feel guilty at times and would chastise myself for being so selfish about having to give up such pleasures as privacy and spontaneous intimacy... but we discovered as we went along these are very real issues and considerations for anyone who decides to become a foster parent.

I could hear the toaster pop up..... then silence, then pop up, again and again. I grabbed my robe and half asleep stumbled into the kitchen. What a surprise. There on the counter top all lined up were ten to twelve slices of toast, each neatly buttered and with about 1/2 inch of jam on each one. As soon as he saw me Lyn stuttered, "Oh these are for Brent and me." (Brent was fast asleep in his crib). Not to embarrass him, I said, "Oh, well Brent is still asleep, but, you know Lyn you can have as much as you want to eat, and you are welcome to help yourself to anything, but please don't make anymore than you are sure you can eat." I then retired back to my bedroom to rest a few minutes more before my husband and Brent would wake up.

This was the beginning of a long series of learning experiences for us in dealing with foster children. Food is a major issue with most of these children. Lyn would be the first in our home, but not the last who would feel the necessity to "store up food" for himself. When a child has experienced true hunger, not having enough to eat, nor any food in the house, his survival instincts kick in. Over the years we would have children who would hide food under their beds, or mattresses, in the garage, in the closet, or even in their school back packs.

In order to reassure the children they would be provided for and there would always be enough food to eat, we would give the child a drawer of his own in the kitchen and put snacks in it and he would be allowed to take from the drawer anytime he felt the need.

Once he realized there was a food source available, the need to steal, hoard or hide food would slowly dissipate. This process could take anywhere from 1 day to several weeks, and some severe cases, months.

It was a blustery, cold day in Portland and on this particular morning we decided we would have oatmeal for breakfast. However, when the bowl was given to Lynden he looked away and then shyly asked, "Could I just have some toast or something?" Jay inquired "Is there something wrong, Lyn?" Reluctantly, he shared his story with us.

Lyn's father, an alcoholic, abandoned Lyn and his four siblings. His mother was dying with cancer and, during her last days, she shared an almost empty apartment with her 5 children. Lyn's sister was 15, he was 14, and there was a 10-year-old and 4-year-old twins. Having nothing besides a twenty-five pound bag of Quaker oats, which had been given to them, for several weeks, his mother and the children had eaten oatmeal for breakfast, lunch and dinner. Lynden just could not face another bowl of oats.

Wealth or poverty is quite dependent on one's point of reference. Lynden felt he had come to live with "rich people" when he came to us. At this time we had a small, 760 square foot home with three bedrooms, one bath and a "step saver" kitchen, but to this boy, who had used newspapers to cover his siblings when they had no heat, we were the "rich people."

Lyn proved to be a wonderful addition to our family. He helped wherever and whenever he could. He worked hard at school, and managed to receive average grades. We received $82/month for his care and on our limited budget this reimbursement money was a welcome asset. Lynden was also to become a wonderful blessing to our family in other ways.

As so often happens, no longer concentrating on having another child, I became pregnant shortly after Brent turned three. My new doctor assured me with this much time lapse between pregnancies there was not that much risk involving my RH-negative type blood. We were very encouraged and looked forward to the new addition to the family.

Our sweet little Janelle was born January 17, 1966. She was so beautiful with her curly strawberry blonde hair and blue eyes.... She looked so perfect. However, on the third day after her birth, I was scheduled to go home and the doctor came in to see me. "We seem to be having a little problem with your baby," he said.... "She has been turning blue in the night, and we'd like to keep her here another day or so, just to observe her." My heart just sank. We would leave the hospital and our precious baby girl would stay behind. The next day, however, Dr. Miracle called and said, "You can take your baby home now. I think she just has a floppy epiglottis and was not getting enough oxygen. She seems to be doing all right." The story of Janelle's life is really another book, but the "lack of oxygen" in her early days has affected her learning ability all of her life.

Janelle never did crawl (which we were to learn later is an absolute must for proper developmental and physical development of a child)... she just rolled anywhere she wanted to go. At about 12 months she did pull herself up, but would not walk. We grew more and more concerned about her slow motor development, and by now had taken her to a pediatric specialist. She would also on occasion roll her eyes back in her head and clinch her fists. We were to learn years later that these had been mini-mal seizures. The pediatrician said we should watch her, but did not offer any further advice.

Now about Lynden and our miracle. About this time, when Janelle was 12 months old, Lynden, who was now 16, began a practice, which probably did more for our baby girl than we ever realized. Each afternoon when he would come home from school, he would drop his books on the kitchen table and look for Janelle. He would then grab her by the straps on her overalls and "walk" her all over the house. The little curly haired blonde pixie giggled with glee when Lyn played this game with her each afternoon. Walkie- walkie to the kitchen, walkie-walkie to the living room, etc. His patience and perseverance paid off when finally, at around 15 months, Janelle took her first steps. Lynden persisted with this exercise for several more months until Janelle could walk on her own. Of course we were not aware at the time that Lynden's desire to help our little daughter, stemmed from a deeper concern and sense of loss for his own little twin brother and sister who had been taken from him. Years later he would pursue searching for them, but to this date we do not know if he ever found them. I am convinced, however, that had Lyn not worked so diligently with Janelle in teaching her and walking her, she would not have developed as well as she has. This young man certainly was an "angel unaware" sent to us from heaven above.

Lyn stayed with us until he graduated from high school and then he entered the Marine Corps. He received a medical discharge due to an allergy to bee stings. He became a successful business owner, married a young woman from the church, and they have 4 children, and reside in Oregon. He will always have a special place in our hearts.

Tommy

"Mrs. Jeffers, we have a little boy we'd like you to meet. He is 3 years old and his name is Tommy."

A more handsome child you will never find than little Tommy. When Brent was 5, Janelle 2 and Lynden 17, we received another call from Social Services. With beautiful thick dark brown hair, and the biggest, dark brown eyes, and olive complexion, we instantly fell in love with this little wisp of a boy. We were told he was French-Indian. I especially remember loving to dress Tommy and Brent alike… their little suits, bow ties and shiny black leather shoes for church. Tommy was very shy, sweet, and such a somber little boy. At first he did not smile very much. We did not know much about his background, other than his mother had turned him over to social services stating she could no longer care for him. He and Brent quickly formed a "brotherly bond" that was to last for 2 years. Since Janelle suffered from allergies and was such a fragile child, it was nice for Brent to have Tommy to play with. Lynden immediately took on the role of "big brother." He was such help with all of the children. I did not ask him for help; he just pitched right in and entertained them, played with them, and thoroughly enjoyed assisting with their care.

It was shear delight to sit at my kitchen table, or out on the patio and watch Brent and Tommy playing their games. Tommy soon relaxed and was just a "regular" kid enjoying the wonders of boyhood. They would hike, and climb and build things. I enjoyed making little costumes for them for their make believe. They loved cowboy and Indian outfits, complete with stick horses made from broomsticks and a stuffed sock with buttons sewn on for the horses heads. I would gather large cardboard boxes from the supermarket and they would use these to build their forts. I would also hang blankets over the clothesline for them to use for tents. The trick was to keep "Rita" our rat terrier from tugging at the blankets and tearing down the tents. Janelle would sometimes join in on the rough and tumble play of the boys, but most of the time she enjoyed her own quiet play with her dolls and her kitten. This was such a happy time for all of us.

By this time we had sold our little house and bought a somewhat larger home with a huge backyard in Troutdale, Oregon. The children had a third acre to play on, complete with swing sets, slides, pets, etc. The neighbor behind us, a minister, and his wife had three little children. They had moved out to Troutdale so their children could have a taste of "country" living. Their backyard was a virtual wonderland to our children, with their little hen house, the chickens, ducks, and even a squirrel or two. Their three children and ours often played together. I remember how Nancy would invite all the children over to help her gather the eggs, and they would eagerly wait their turns to scatter grain for the animals.

Nancy never asked, but I assumed she wondered about my two blond- haired, blue-eyed children and then Tommy, who was olive skinned with dark hair and eyes. One day over coffee I told her that we were foster parents and that Tommy was our foster child. She smiled and said, "Oh, I think it is so wonderful. What a lucky boy Tommy is to have you." Up until that time I had not thought of it quite that way. I always thought how lucky we were to have Tommy. Quite often when I would sit in my kitchen and look out the window at the children playing together I would fantasize Tommy was actually ours. I never considered the possibility someday he might be taken from us. I believed God had given us this child for a reason, and someday He would reveal that to us. But for now, I was just content to know this precious little boy was part of our family.

When Tommy was almost 5 his social worker asked us if we might be interested in adopting him. We were stunned. Back in the 60's foster parents were discouraged completely from even thinking about adopting their foster children. Thank goodness that time and education have changed this way of thinking. Today the National standard is the extended family are first and then the current foster parents are the next ones to be asked if they would like to adopt their foster children. I recently heard 80% of the adoptions in Nevada, where we currently reside, are by foster parents who adopt their foster children. We didn't have to think about it very long. Tommy had become an integral part of our family. We loved him as our own, and could not bear the thought of him having to go to another family. We eagerly said we would be happy to adopt him. The social worker said she would get the ball rolling. We were so thrilled about having this precious little boy as our own. We began preparing our extended family members to receive this little boy into the family. Since he had been with us for over 2 years this was very easy for everyone... we all loved him so.

We will never forget the day we received the call. "Mrs. Jeffers, there is a new development in the adoption of Tommy we need to discuss with you." The sound of her voice gave away her concern and immediately something inside me just died. Intuition is a powerful force, especially when it concerns a mother and her child. It would come into play many times over the years, as we would deal with the ups and downs, the negatives and positives, the triumphs and the tragedies we would experience in caring for our foster children.

Just as it is today, back in 1968, Social Services, before terminating a parent's rights and placing a child for adoption, must send out a letter to all family members and relatives, regardless of how distant, informing them of the legal actions that are taking place. Such a letter went out to Tommy's biological father's home and was received by his wife. She was shocked to receive this letter informing her that, while she and her husband Tom were separated, he had fathered a child with a much younger woman. Unbeknownst to him the young woman had later abandoned the child to social services. Tommy's father and wife, whom I will call Mary, had four daughters and were now reconciled. When Mary, who is a very devout Catholic, learned that Tom, who had now returned to her and their daughters, had a son who was in foster care, she determined this child belonged with his natural father and her. This, no matter how painful to us, was to prove to be the best outcome for Tommy.

We met over the next few months with Tom and Mary and they turned out to be wonderful people who had gone through a very rough time, but were now determined to have their family whole and together.

I can remember their first visit with Tommy as if it happened yesterday. The social worker had arranged for an unsupervised visit and Tommy's parents, Tom and Mary had called to set a time. They would be here Saturday morning at 11:00 a.m. and take Tommy to lunch. That whole week I had been preparing Tommy for the visit and for meeting his "new mommy" and his biological father whom he had not seen since he was an infant, and of whom he had absolutely no recollection. "But you and dad are my mommy and daddy," he protested. Somehow I must convey to him that he had a biological father and a new mother who were eager to have him as part of their family. I must do this very carefully so he would not think we were abandoning him... the greatest fear of any child, and especially one who has already experienced the pain of abandonment.

"Tommy, do you remember that time when you lost little Teddy?" Little Teddy was a ragged stuffed bear Tommy had picked out from our "toy drawer" the first day he arrived at our house. Little Teddy was taken everywhere and at one time even had the pleasure of a bubble bath...followed of course by a trip to the clothes dryer. He had been pulled from the jaws of our rat terrier, "Rita," and rescued from the limbs of the oak tree in the front yard, where a neighborhood bully had mean spiritedly thrown him. Little Teddy was Tommy's constant companion, and on many occasions had soaked up the tears of a frightened child or been the "ear" who listened to a disgruntled boy or girl. "Yes," he replied, "I remember when he got lost and we found him at the bottom of the clothes hamper." "Well, do you remember how happy you were after you thought Teddy was lost and you searched for him, and you asked the rest of the family to look for him, and several days later he was found?" "Oh yes," he chirped, his big brown eyes wide with remembrance, "I was so happy, like I'd found a treasure!" "Well, Tommy" I continued, "Your real daddy and mommy have been searching for you, and now they are so happy that they have found you. "You are like a lost treasure to them." "Oh," he replied, "how did they lose me." I was taken back by such honest questioning from this innocent little child. "They can tell you all about it after you get to know them, Tommy," I replied, "And I'm sure they'll be happy to answer any questions you have." Could this five year old child really understand the significance of "being lost" and now "being found," when I myself often questioned how adults could "lose" their children, the greatest treasure with which any of us will ever be blessed.

Tom and Mary arrived right on time, 11:00 a.m. Saturday morning. We were curious to meet this couple who were now invading our lives and threatening to take our precious Tommy from us. I must admit, however, we were pleasantly surprised when we opened the door and there stood a very average, pleasant looking middle aged couple obviously of modest means who greeted us very cordially. Mary stood about 5'8" slightly taller than her husband, and had brown, with a few streaks of gray, shoulder length hair. She was dressed in a crisp, neatly ironed, flower print dress, with a pale pink cardigan sweater. Tom wore brown pants, neatly creased, an open collared long sleeve checked pullover shirt, which had been very neatly ironed, his shoes were polished with care, and his thinning hair slicked back. Mary was obviously a woman who took great pride in the appearance of her family. Jay invited them in and offered them a seat on the couch.

What I expected to be an awkward moment surprisingly was not awkward at all. Mary thanked us for inviting them over and said how very eager they were to see little Tommy. She had previously shared over the phone with me how it had come about that she and her husband, who had 4 girls ranging in age from twelve to twenty-two had separated when Tom ran off with a younger woman. She had been totally unaware he had fathered a child. There was no need to discuss this again during the visit so Jay went to get Tommy without any further delay.

He looked so cute, all dressed up in his Sunday best. He was wearing his little brown suit with the matching vest, a long sleeved dress shirt and a little brown bow tie. I cannot remember how many times that morning I had combed and re-combed his thick wavy hair. Jay brought him into the living room and at first he clung to Jay's leg, but then he stepped forward and looked at these two strangers and said "Hi, my name's Tommy."

I often wondered what thoughts must have gone through Mary's mind the first time she met her husband's "love child." Tommy looked nothing like either Mary or Tom, who both had very fair complexions. Mary was tall and average build and Tom was short and stocky. When Mary looked at Tommy did she see the "other woman" who must have had dark brown hair and big brown eyes and a slender build? If she did she certainly did not show it. Immediately, I could see the love in her eyes as she looked at Tommy for the first time. This was the son she and Tom had never had together. This was the son of the man she had loved and cherished for over 25 years and who was the father of their four daughters. This was the boy who was lost and now had been found. This little boy was to become her son.

The resilience of children in foster care never ceases to amaze us. Outrageous requests are made of them, and they respond with such amazing strength. Here was 5-year-old Tommy, leaving the comfort of the only home he had known for two years, the family he had come to love and trust, and going off with, for all practical purposes, total strangers to have lunch and answer questions he had no way of anticipating. What a little trooper he was. The picture of him walking down the walkway between these two people, glancing back over his shoulder at me with those big, brown, questioning eyes will be forever etched in my memory.

Tommy did not say much following the first visit with his "real" parents. When we asked him if he'd had a nice time he just shook his head and said "Uh, huh"…and that was it.

This was not to be the case with subsequent visits. The next weekend Tommy was to go home with his parents and meet his four older sisters for the first time. The picture of him returning home after the visit, bouncing up the walkway, laughing cheerfully, and his excitement as he told us about a house in the country with chickens, ducks, and even a pony for him to ride was an unexpected occurrence. He shared how he had milked a cow and baked bread with his sisters. They had missed him very much and were all so happy to see him.

His little face just lit up with enthusiasm as he shared with us the wonderful weekend he had spent on the "farm." "My daddy misses me so much," he gushed "and he is so happy I will be coming home. But does this mean I will have to leave you?"

Deep down inside each one of us, I believe, is a space we reserve for those very personal, never to be shared, darkest, deepest thoughts. Some of them may even be on the evil side, and some of them just fantasies… but there is such a reservoir, a place where we push those thoughts that are too hideous, outrageous, or personal, to hold in our memory. It is from this cavern in our soul that I am sure my thoughts crept out at this time. As much as I had prayed that, if it were God's will for Tommy to be reunited with his parents, it would happen smoothly and without incident, still down deep in my soul there was this secret hope it might not happen. As I witnessed him begin to re-attach to his long lost family, and establish a rapport with them and then even, yes, look forward to their visits I could feel jealousy and even spite welling up within me.

Secretly there was always this little thread of hope perhaps they would not want Tommy in the end, or his father would default in payment of his newly court-ordered child care payments. Tom had not paid childcare since Tommy's disappearance from his life. The court was now requiring him to contribute to his son's care. The court was testing his resolve and commitment to get his son back and provide for him. Tom did not default, however, Mary made sure of that, and they fulfilled every requirement and request the State courts asked of them in reestablishing a relationship with their son. They visited him on a regular basis, called when they said they would, and were so very careful and gentle in communicating with Tommy and with us. They dotted every "I" and crossed every "t" social services demanded of them to meet their obligations with the State.

The State social worker advised us Tommy would soon be going home to live with his biological family. Mary was very understanding of our feelings regarding our pending loss of Tommy. She told us she would be happy for us to visit Tommy and receive photos of him as he grew up. Four months later we were to pack up our little boy's belongings, and after a tearful good-bye, hugs and kisses, we placed our little Tommy in the arms of his new mommy and his biological father. They thanked us repeatedly for the care we had given him, and apologized for breaking our hearts.

Feeling as though we had been dragged by a freight train and absolutely drained from crying and the grief associated with losing a child, it was at this time we vowed never again to take in foster children, to love them so deeply, and suffer the broken heart that comes with losing them. We kept in touch with Tommy's family for about a year and he quickly adapted into his new family, it was then we decided to step back and let him get on with his new life. We knew he was where he belonged; he was home! His picture is still in our family album and he will always be in our hearts.

A lesson we were to learn over and over is, although we know in most instances we can provide a better home, more supervision, material things, spiritual guidance, unconditional love, and other advantages in the lives of our foster children, deep inside each child has an innate desire to be with his or her biological family. No matter how much neglect or disadvantage these children suffer, there is still that powerful instinct to be with one's own family. The exception to this, of course, is in some cases of severe sexual or physical abuse and abandonment.

Dale

It was 3:15 p.m. and, as the phone rang, I felt a real sense of sadness come over me. Should I answer it? School was out and he would be walking home, dejectedly, so alone and not wanting to go home to "her." His dad was on the road and there was no one he could talk to. I knew there would be a little voice at the other end, pleading "Mommy, please can I come back and live with you? Please! Mommy, she is so mean to me and now David has been put in detention and I'm all alone. I miss you, mommy, and I want to come home." He had been calling every day, but this day I would not, must not answer. I slowly turned and walked away, the salty tears trickled from my eyes... no, I must not answer... turn the radio on... the ringing stopped, finally.

Hello, Mrs. Jeffers, this is Ms. Thompson from Social Services. I know you have taken a leave from foster care, however; there is a little boy I would like you to meet. His name is Dale and he's at Dorenbecher Children's Hospital. He is ready to be released but we cannot find a suitable placement for him. Would you be willing to at least meet me at the hospital and let me introduce you to Dale? He is 9 years old.

Reluctantly, and maybe somewhat from curiosity, an inner excitement crept in and I decided to meet with this Ms. Thompson and see who this little boy Dale was, who now resided at Children's Hospital. It is my belief one element in foster care, if I am completely honest, one reason we became foster parents, is a genuine desire to know and learn about others who share the planet with us. I love to learn about individuals, where they come from, what their family members are like, the way their home is decorated. Some may call it just being nosey, but to me it is a genuine interest in others. Ms. Thompson introduced me to Dale. He had blonde hair, blue eyes, a slight build, a beautiful smile and a real twinkle in his eye. Immediately I was hooked. Now I must convince Jay.

Other than our vow never again to take in a child or to have our hearts broken, Jay and I had not spoken in depth regarding foster care since Tommy's departure. Neither one of us wanted to bring up the subject because it would mean dealing with the pain of losing Tommy. During the short time since Tommy's return to his parents I often found myself thinking about having another child in our home. Then there would be that "check" in my spirit and the question would arise, "Do you really want to have your heart broken again?" I could also see Brent really missed his little foster brother and playmate. We did not realize until years later how insecure losing Tommy must have made Brent feel. In his little mind he reasoned children could just be taken from their parents and never returned.

It was during this post grief period also I began to see fostering children possibly as a "calling." I believe all of us are here to serve a higher purpose and we all must contribute to making the world a better place to live. Before fostering children I was not sure just what my role would be.

After meeting Dale, seeing the desperate need he had to be nurtured and cared for, I reached my decision. It was during this decision making process that I remembered a book I had read years ago. It was titled "Let my Heart Be Broken " and the author, who worked with starving and orphaned children in third world countries, stated in serving others there is quite often a great price to pay, and the price is that of a broken heart. The author had also determined for himself to "let my heart be broken with the things that break the heart of God." This would become my credo. There were no lights flashing, nor bells ringing. This was just a "this is what I must do" type of decision. Fostering children is the right thing to do and it is something I can do here and now to help alleviate human suffering. I was so pleased when Jay agreed with me wholeheartedly. I did not even have the challenge of convincing him. Jay is very tenderhearted in considering the needs of others. This is why, in later years, he would become a very effective marriage and family counselor.

The next day, complete with a large black garbage bag containing his belongings, Dale came home from the hospital and would be with us for the next 10 months. For all he had been through, Dale was the most delightful, cheerful, eager-to-please little fellow you could ever hope to meet. Jay immediately replaced the beds in the boys' room with bunk beds. Dale would sleep on top and Brent on the bottom. Janelle now had her own room, and Lyn had gone off to the Marine Corps.

That evening, while getting the boys ready for bed, I saw the horrible evidence of the abuse that had been inflicted on this little 9-year-old boy and the reason he had been removed from his home. There on his chest and shoulders were large splash- like scars. These hideous scars were from burns caused when Dale's stepmother poured scalding water on him. While he was in the kitchen doing dishes, Dale and his older brother, David, were splashing water, which angered his stepmother. Consequently, she picked up a pan of water that had been boiling on the stove and dumped it on him. It brought tears to my eyes to think of the tremendous pain this little boy had endured. Afraid of being found out, the step-mother did not seek medical help for him. It was not until neighbors saw the seeping sores on his body caused by infection and called the police department that Dale was picked up and received treatment for his third degree burns. There were weeks in the hospital with skin graft operations and all of the pain associated with burns and infection. This little boy endured this alone. No mother to hold, comfort him and reassure him that everything was going to be all right. If the truth were known, Dale probably actually thought he deserved these burns and he worried he would be in trouble for causing so much inconvenience to his step-mom.

Dale's father, I'll call him John, was a truck driver and was gone from home two to three weeks each month. John had previously been married and had two little boys, Dale and his brother David. Their mother had died very young of an aneurysm and John was left with two little boys to raise. He re-married and he and his new wife, I'll call Susan, had two more children.

Susan resented John's children by his previous marriage and began neglecting them. She would place fresh fruit on the table and tell them, "This is for "my" children and you are not to touch it." Is it any wonder that several years later Dale's brother, David, wound up needing psychiatric care and eventually landed in the juvenile justice system?

We always took the children to church and they all enjoyed learning about the love of their heavenly father. Although Social Services discouraged parents from teaching religion to foster children, we felt God had placed these children with us and we answered to a higher authority. We knew these children needed strength beyond their own to get them through the circumstances and tragedies in their lives, so they were included in all of the church services. As long as the biological parents did not protest, Social Services did not object. Music has always managed to reach the depths of my soul, and so it is no wonder tears would come to my eyes as I would hear their precious little voices singing, "Jesus loves me this I know, for the Bible tells me so. Little ones to Him belong, they are weak but He is strong."

It was a rainy afternoon, the wind was blowing, and the four of us were all cuddled up on the couch Brent on one side of me, Dale on the other and Janelle sitting on my lap. Reading stories was a special time for all of us, and the children seemed to delight in hearing the same stories over and over. It was on occasions like this when I noticed how Dale would sometimes curl up, almost in a fetal position, and tuck his head under the blanket and occasionally suck his thumb. Even though he was nine years old, for some reason I did not feel prompted to correct this behavior. Although, having no training in child development or dealing with children with anxiety or separation disorders, something within me told me Dale needed the comfort of cuddling up to "mommy," being nurtured and being allowed to suck his thumb. Eventually I just slowly removed his thumb from his mouth and then I would rub his head, and run my fingers through his hair. He would cuddle up ever so close to me and look up at me with those big blue eyes and say, "Mommy, I love you."

It was at times like these, with my own two children safe beside me that I could not help but think about Dale's biological mother. She had died so young and been taken from her children when they were just babies. They did not experience the benefit of the cuddling and the nestling and all that comes with the nurturing that takes place between a mother and child. She must have been a pretty woman as both of her children had such nice features, beautiful fair complexions, blue eyes and delightful personalities. How broken hearted she would have been to know that her husband, desperately needing a mother for his children, had re-married to a woman who would reject and then neglect and abuse these little ones. I remember speaking a silent vow to Dale's deceased mother saying, "As long as God allows me, I will take care of your little boy, and love and nurture him the way you would have wanted to, and the way in which he deserves."

Against his will, very reluctantly Dale did go home on weekly visitations and, unfortunately, he would make comments to his stepmother, Susan, that irritated her and she let me know about it. Evidently Dale would remark to her how he liked it better at our house because he did not get yelled at or hit… our house was clean, and there weren't beer bottles all over the place. When Susan brought Dale back to our house following his visit she yelled at me from the porch "You have no business teaching my kids about God and criticizing my life-style. I do not want you taking Dale to church anymore… I want nothing to do with God or your religion. When I get him back I'll change his mind. You can be sure of it." We had never criticized her life style. We know better than to do this because so often the children are returned to the parents and we don't want them to be embarrassed about their home situation.

Even though we try never to comment to the children about the home environment they have been removed from, they do recognize the difference between living in chaos and disorder, and living in peace and harmony. Many children at first will try to re-create the dissention and chaos they have come out of. However, once they adapt to a peaceful environment, regular meal and bath schedules and a routine bedtime, they begin to relax and their behavior begins to change. They realize not everyone lives in constant disruption, disorganization, people coming and going all hours of the night, and in abusive situations. They begin to learn how a more reasonable family functions.

One week later when Dale's dad, John, came for him for a bi-weekly visit, I greeted him at the door and he lowered his head and said apologetically, "I am so sorry for the things Susan said to you. I am in such a tough place. She is good to our other two children, and I am gone so much of the time, and I just do not know what to do about the way she treats Dale and David. The court has ordered her into counseling and we are going together when I am home. Anyway, I appreciate your care of Dale and you have my permission to take him to church. We need all the help we can get."

Six months later the court deemed Dale's home suitable for his return. His stepmother had completed the necessary counseling and assured the court she was prepared to be a better, more responsible parent to him. I would be lying if I didn't say I had serious doubts. Dale would always return to us from his home visits with reports of "no food in the house," "no clean clothes to wear" and "no supervision." At 9 years of age, on many occasions his mother would leave him alone in charge of his two younger siblings. The courts had decided though and it was now out of our hands. Reluctantly, we packed up his belongings. His social worker came to pick him up to return him to his home a few days later. He begged the caseworker "Please let me stay here, I don't want to leave." It was so painful as he clung to me and cried "I want to stay with you mommy, don't make me go back there!!" I cried bitterly that night, as I knew, unless something changed Susan's heart, Dale would be at risk.

He called me several times after that, and would ask, "Mommy, can I come home to you and dad?" It broke my heart to tell him, "No, Dale, you must stay in your own home but you know you are in our hearts and we think of you and pray for you every day."

A few weeks later the phone calls stopped. We do not know what happened to Dale after that. We can only wish for him the 10 months in our home gave him a model of what a loving, caring, nurturing family is so when he is grown he will be able to have that kind of family and home for himself, his wife and his children.

Howard

"There's got to be a special place in hell for people who would do something like this to a child!" This became a "cliché" of mine and one I tapered off from somewhat over the years. With education and experience I learned quite often abusive parents were the victims of childhood abuse themselves. This is a learned behavior and one we as a society must work to abolish. We must stop the chain of violence.

Somehow knowing this brought little consolation in knowing what had happened to Howard.

He was such a sad, forlorn looking little boy. Howard was just 5 and Brent was 6 when Social Services dropped him off at our door. He was wearing a tattered shirt, filthy sweat pants, no socks, and shoes much too large for his feet. His long black hair was disheveled and he looked at me through hollow, coal black eyes. He had a stocky build and we discovered he was very strong.

"I'm sorry Ms. Jeffers for bringing him here in this condition, but I had no place else to take him." We brought him straight to you from the police station. Again, the black garbage bag with a few of his tattered belongings thrown inside. Later in the week I threw out all of his clothing. It reeked of urine. I figured he must have wet himself and then his clothes would be stripped off and tossed into the dryer without being washed. No amount of bleaching or hanging out in the sunshine would remove the stench of the urine.

Fortunately Howard was just about the same size as Brent so I grabbed some suitable clothing from Brent's drawers and closets and after a good hot bath and shampoo, the little boy was all fresh and clean and no longer smelled of urine.

In the 60s and 70's, Social Services still considered a child's history and record as "confidential" so foster parents were not given much information regarding the child being placed in their care. With Howard's bizarre behaviors however, little bits and pieces began to fit together like a puzzle. I asked, and the caseworker began to share with me some of his background so I could be prepared for and know how to respond to his behavior.

Howard was terrified of the dark and would scream out if the lights were turned off. We immediately put a night light in his room and in the bathroom. As his story unfolded we learned this little boy had repeatedly been locked in a dark closet by his parents and left for hours on end, sometimes for as long as two days. He would have no choice but to urinate and defecate in the closet he was occupying. He became dehydrated and sick and vomited on himself and his clothing. When his parents returned home following their spree of drinking and gambling, he would be taken from the closet and severely punished for the "mess" he had made. He would be thrown into a cold shower, with his clothes on, and told "Clean yourself up you little worthless piece of dung."

While changing Howard's clothes we also noticed little nickel-sized round scars all over his chest, legs, arms, back and buttocks. I brought this to the attention of the caseworker and after their investigation we were told she learned from interviewing Howard's mother that his father would come home drunk at night. He would then light up a cigar and in his drunken stupor he would drag Howard out of bed and proceed to burn him with the end of cigar. At first he would cry out in pain and his father retaliated by bashing him across the head. Eventually when his father would burn him, Howard would not even cry out. This is, I'm sure, where he developed that dark, hollow stare. Mentally he would just go to another place and endure the pain in silence. He was only 5 years old.

Why didn't his mother protect him? This is a question we have too often had to ask ourselves regarding children who have been abused. Where are the mothers whose duty it is to nurture and protect their children? What happens to a woman that would cause her to abdicate her utmost responsibility and her natural born instinct to protect her young? In recent years, as drug addiction and alcohol have been brought into the equation of dysfunctional families and child abuse, neglect and abandonment, we have discovered the reasons for this dilemma.

Brent, in his friendly, unselfish, non-judgmental, loving ways, quickly adopted Howard as his new brother. He did not hesitate to share his toys nor his time with this new, angry, beaten down addition to our family. We were sure that with time, provision, and unconditional love and security, Howard would begin to respond.

This is where we learned another very difficult and disheartening lesson. There is a point at which there is no return. With enough abuse, neglect, torture, starvation, humiliation and abandonment, a child can retreat into himself to a place where you cannot bring him back. This was the sad result in Howard's case. It seemed that no amount of holding, talking, or encouragement could get through to Howard. We just could not reach him. Today there are resources provided for abused children. There are therapists, psychologists, psychiatrists, and pediatricians to assist and advise in the treatment of these little victims. This was not the case in 1970. It was left up to us, the foster parents and the caseworkers, to work with these children. Howard was beyond the scope of our expertise. I am saddened to write that eventually the emotional toll and expended energy were just too great for our family to bear. We were not equipped to respond to the needs of this badly damaged little boy. When he began biting, hitting and kicking the other children, and ultimately threatening others with a knife, for the safety of the rest of the family members, we requested Howard be removed from our home. Unfortunately, at that time the only alternative was institutionalization. We have no way of knowing his outcome, but it certainly seemed bleak.

Howard was a victim and living example of man's inhumanity to man. "Oh, Howard, how our hearts break for you. If our love could have healed you, you would be well. You were so broken, we did not know how to put you back together again."

Once again we learned a valuable lesson in our journey along the path of foster care. We cannot fix every child who is broken. Some conditions are strictly beyond our ability and control. We can, however, dedicate ourselves to learning everything we can about the human psyche, and avail ourselves of all the knowledge and tools available to assist us in the care of these little lives. Today there are professionals specially trained in the treatment of abused and neglected children. We must advocate and mediate for the innocent ones. We can cry out until our voices are heard and society responds to the needs of the less fortunate. We can and must continue to improve in our efforts to provide a safe haven for the children.

In the area of Mental Health and Substance Abuse, the *National Fact Sheet 2012* provided the following statistics, which are of interest.
- The U.S. Department of Health and Human Services estimates that 75%-80% of children who need mental health services do not receive them.
- More than 80% of children in foster care have developmental, emotional, or behavioral problems. Mental health services are repeatedly identified as their number one health care need.
- Suicide is the third leading cause of death among teen and young adults. In 2000, 3,994 teens and young adults ages 15-24 committed suicide—one every 2 hours and 12 minutes.
- Severe mental illness is highly correlated with alcohol and other drug dependence or abuse. In 2002, among adults with severe mental illness, 23.2% were dependent on or abused alcohol or other drugs. The rate among adults without severe mental illness was only 8.2%
- In 2001, approximately 6.1 million children lived with parents who abused alcohol and other drugs. Of these, 1.1 million were younger than 3.

After Howard's departure we vowed we would try to be more selective with the children we agreed to have placed in our home. Howard had literally sucked all of the energy out of both of us. We decided to take a rest and vowed to spend more time with Brent and Janelle. We bought a little camper for our truck and began taking camping trips to the beach and to the mountains. Our family had always enjoyed the outdoors and camping fit both our need for recreation and our budget. Evenings spent by a campfire roasting hot dogs and making s'mores were to become a way of life with us. To this day, when offered a choice of vacation ideas, my first choice will always be a camping trip up the Oregon coast, a few days at Harris Beach with walks along the shore, dining on clam chowder at the Dory Cove, and falling asleep to the crashing of the waves. The ocean is very therapeutic to me. Standing in awe of the immensity and dimension of the sea, my heart says, "If God can control the ocean, certainly He can take care of His children."

Lonnie

"Virginia, " called my neighbor Frieda, "Can I speak with you for just a moment?"

"Sure," I said, "Just let me grab Janelle and I'll be right over." "Now I don't want you to think I am complaining," Frieda went on, "and it's really quite all right with me, but I just thought you ought to know Lonnie has been coming into our garage and taking apples." I appreciated the fact she did not say he was "stealing" apples. "Now I want you to know that he can have all the apples he wants, but we just don't want him to waste them." Lonnie had been stuffing his pockets with apples from my neighbor's garage. Further investigation turned up apples, oranges, bananas, half-filled boxes of crackers, cookies, rotten left over pizza, and other food items, which were now collecting mold, in such places as Lonnie's pillowcase, under his bed, in his drawers, and hidden in our garage. Lonnie was storing up food in preparation for a time when he thought he might be denied food as a means of punishment or just plain neglect.

Lonnie, too, had arrived on our doorstep with a large garbage bag in one hand and a toy truck in the other. He was giggling and wiggling and just could not stand still. You would not have guessed he had been picked up at 11:00 p.m. the night before, spent the night in the police station while the authorities tried to locate his mother, had fallen asleep under a policeman's desk and was now being delivered to our house by the first available case worker on the scene. Brent was now 8 and Lonnie, though about two inches taller than Brent was just 7. He was a stocky little guy, with a big round face, big brown eyes and uncontrollable dark brown hair. Had he been evaluated at that time, as he would be if he were coming into the foster care system today, I'm sure they would have diagnosed him as either FASD (Fetal Alcohol Syndrome Disorder) or ADHD (Attention Deficit Hyperactivity Disorder). This kid was like a spinning top. It was go, go, go. He had one speed and that was fast. He talked constantly and was like a wind up toy with the main spring broken. He WAS the energizer bunny. Lonnie would wake up at the crack of dawn and was like a tornado all day until he crashed at night. Everything he did, he did with a vengeance. He played hard, laughed hard, ate as much as any adult, and was so loud. He slammed doors, slid down the banister, tripped over his own feet, and fell out of trees. He was likeable, laughable and lovable. He was also very insecure.

There was another incident, one of many, involving food. The local corner grocery store manager called me to report Lonnie had been in the market and filled his pockets with candy bars, sandwiches, and peanuts. He then ran out of the store as fast as he could. The manager was satisfied when the items not yet eaten were returned and we paid for the already consumed items. Even after months of living with us in a safe environment with three meals a day, plus snacks and treats, Lonnie never could get past the temptation of stealing and hoarding food. At school he often got in trouble for taking other kids' lunches, even when he had an adequate lunch provided for him.

The Cub Scouts were a Godsend for Lonnie. He and Brent were both enrolled and they thoroughly enjoyed it. Lonnie seemed to relish in the competition and he worked very hard to earn his badges. He was quite adept with tools and Jay and the boys enjoyed building their bird-houses and other projects. Lonnie loved to take things apart and put them together again. Unfortunately, quite often he would take things apart that did not need fixing and he might not be able to re-assemble them. He would be scolded but this did not deter him. He loved to swing a hammer, and when we went camping he wanted to swing the axe. Since he was bound and determined to do it anyway, Jay taught him how to do it safely, and he became our official wood splitter.

The first Christmas Lonnie spent with us he was just like a bull in a china shop. He was so hyper and excited through the whole Christmas season. He kept shaking the presents under the tree and would go almost ballistic when told some of the presents were for him and he could open them Christmas morning. We asked him what he would like for Christmas and he said a bicycle.

At this time Jay was enrolled in Medical Technology School and as before, and for so many years it seemed, we were on such a limited, tight budget. We had our own two children, plus Lonnie and two other emergency placement foster children just before Christmas. We did not know how we would manage financially to provide for all of their needs and wants. Thank you, Lord, for the Portland Fire Department. A dear neighbor of ours, sensing our dilemma over the many needs of the children during the holidays, heard about a program at the local fire department. They took in used bicycles, repaired and repainted them until they were just like new. They gave out these bicycles to needy children. We were contacted shortly before Christmas and asked if we could use a bicycle. "Oh, yes," I replied without hesitating.

Christmas morning when the children came down and saw the tree with all of its many presents they were ecstatic. Under the tree was a brand new bicycle (this one was not refurbished). The fire department had received several new bikes from a local department store. When we told Lonnie it was for him, he went bonkers on us. He did not know what to do. He began jumping up and down and spinning in circles. He tugged at his hair and tossed himself down on the carpet. It was the strangest display of elation we had ever seen. Of course, that bicycle was not three hours old when Lonnie rode it to the local gas station, and, even though it did not need it, he decided to inflate the tires, over-inflated and blew out the rear tire. He was constantly working on that bike. Before it was two months old, it looked like an old used junkyard bike; but he enjoyed every minute of it. He painted it (yep, it was brand new but that didn't stop him), put decals on it, raised and lowered the handlebars, and almost rode it to death. We lost count of how many times he crashed into trees, popped tires going down curbs, rode into a fence, and ran over a cat. He was hell on wheels.

We also learned another lesson that Christmas. Jay's parents were visiting with us and when it was all over and the children had settled down with their presents, my father-in-law commented to us: "You know it looks like your foster children received a lot more than your own children." Sadly, we had to admit it was true. In our eagerness to provide a wonderful Christmas to these needy little children who had come to us, and due to the generosity of the Fire Department who provided wonderful gifts for our foster children, we had not ensured our own children received an equal amount. They had each received little gifts, but nothing so wonderful as a bicycle. I felt a tremendous sense of guilt, and right then and there I vowed never to make the same mistake again.

A common concern among foster care providers who have children of their own is learning to provide the proper balance between the care given to foster children, most of whom are so needy, and care of your own biological children. We tended to lean towards the opposite end of the spectrum. We would then feel guilty for expending so much time and energy on the foster children that we felt we were neglecting our own children. I would then console myself with the fact my own children had so much. They had their own parents who loved and cared for them, they had a warm home and security and love, and all of the advantages the foster children didn't. We did learn the old adage "robbing Peter to pay Paul" could also apply here. It was not fair to diminish the time and energy spent with our own children to meet the needs of the unfortunate. If we did not have the time or energy to devote to our own children, we had no business taking on additional responsibilities. We worked at it, and with considerable practice, learned to maintain an equitable balance.

Our son, Brent, reassured us he never felt slighted or put aside because of the foster children who came into our home. The eternal optimist, he says "It was no sacrifice, mom. I never was alone and I always had lots of kids to play with. It was so much fun. I really felt sorry for the circumstances some of these kids came out of and I was glad we could share with them. It made me happy."

Janelle, on the other hand, did not fare quite as well I am afraid. In retrospect, with her learning disability, I am convinced more time could and should have been spent with her in those early years. Did I spread myself too thin, and should I have been more aware of her needs? She had a difficult time in school, and we were not to find out until years later just how miserable she was in the eighth grade. She was the one student picked out by the others and bullied. With such a strong desire to help others, had I neglected the one closest to me? This is a question that will haunt me the rest of my life.

We really did not have that much information on Lonnie's background. To our knowledge he had not been categorized as abused, but neglected. To me there is a fine line between the two...and it is hard to define where one crosses over into the next. Lonnie was left on his own to fend for himself. The neighbors would call the authorities when they would see him out wandering the streets late at night, barefoot and without a coat in 30-degree temperatures. Investigation would show either his mother was at the local bar, or she was home, passed out on the couch. The cupboards would be empty and Lonnie would ask the neighbors for food, or scrounge in garbage cans. He was not attending school on a regular basis and when he was there, he was not properly clothed and he had not been fed. Other students complained of him taking their lunches and stealing their milk. This was a classic case of sheer neglect. Lonnie, however, was a survivor.

Over the years, most of the foster children we were to take in came to us in the "survival mode." They would do whatever it took to have their needs met. If it meant stealing, lying, bullying, cheating, they would do it. It is a fact if a child cannot get what he needs through positive means, he will turn to negative behavior to get his needs met. We found this to be true, without exception, in the lives of all of our foster children.

Lonnie was to stay with us another year and a half. At that time his grandmother stepped forward and agreed to provide a home for him. It is amazing how many times this is the case. In this country there are many grandparents assuming the task of raising their grandchildren, either because their children are irresponsible, drug addicted, have made bad choices, or just are not emotionally equipped to raise children. There are now organizations comprised of members who are grandparents raising grandchildren. Many of these generous, caring people have worked all of their lives, but there will be no retirement for them.

Without much fanfare, Lonnie packed his things, vowed to keep in touch, and without tears or long good-byes he left us in the company of his grandmother. He did not look back and we did not hear from him again. Lonnie is just too busy getting on with, and enjoying, life.

Lisa

It's a terrible thing to admit, but at this writing, Lisa is almost a blur to me. She came, she stayed and she left. However, what I do remember about Lisa is the tremendous lesson I learned and how I was forced to deal with my own prejudice.

She was just 7 years old when the Social Worker dropped her off at our home with her garbage bag full of belongings. She had beautiful long hair, was tall for her age, and seemed to have an air of confidence about her. However, we were to discover this was just a façade. Inside, she was a frightened little girl who was confused and afraid. We never did find out why she had been removed from her home or was in the foster care system. Here she was though and she needed someone to care for her. From the beginning Lisa was very dramatic…about everything. She would toss her head around and give commands to the other children. She would flip her hair from side to side and she enjoyed admiring herself in the mirror. She was quite the femme fatale. She had brought a lovely doll with her and made it very clear this belonged to her and no one was to touch it. She would waltz into the room and very properly seat herself at the dinner table. She loved to display her exceptionally good manners and expected others to respond in turn.

It wasn't long though before Lisa's actions really began to annoy me. She seemed to be putting on airs and she became the house "tattle tale." She would run to us with every little misdeed the others would do and wanted to "whisper them in our ear." She almost seemed to delight in seeing the others reprimanded for their shortcomings. She criticized the others if their beds were not perfectly made and she shrieked at anyone who came near any of her possessions. On a couple of occasions I caught her teasing Janelle by taking her toys away and hiding them.

This was when I discovered a truth about myself. I could NOT love all children. It was becoming increasingly hard for me to even like this one. There is no written law that foster parents must love the children they care for. Increasingly I found myself just providing for Lisa's needs and then practically ignoring her afterwards. This, in part, because of the guilt I was feeling for really not liking her. What was wrong with me? This was a poor little child, away from her home and family, in need of reassurance and love, and she was not receiving that from me. I could not even bring myself to "fake it" with Lisa. I shared my feeling with the caseworker and expressed how annoying this little girl was to me. You can imagine my relief when she said, "Oh my dear, none of us can like every child we come in contact with. Some are just more loveable than others and some are almost impossible at times. Good heavens, we can't even like all of our relatives, let alone total strangers." This certainly took the pressure off of me and I gave myself permission not to feel as though I must like every child just because he was a child. This did not mean I could not tend to their needs and provide them with warmth and security and a comfortable place to relax and heal.

I also learned that, for me, raising boys is much easier than raising girls. Boys will be loud, rough, tumbly, noisy, rude, crass and nasty. But with boys, what you see is what you get. They let it "all hang out." Boys are also more inclusive with other boys. If two boys are playing ball and a third walks up, he is asked to join in. The more the merrier when it comes to the masculine gender. It wasn't so with girls. I found them to be more moody, dramatic, sneaky, gossipy and exclusive. Girls need a "best friend." If two girls are playing and a third one enters the picture, one or the other of the two girls will whisper, "Let's go over to my house and play without her," or "I'll be your best friend if you tell her you can't play right now." Girls are more likely to be jealous of each other and to turn on each other. Boys will defend each other to the end, whereas girls, at least the ones in my care, will tattle on each other and spread gossip. I could write a whole chapter right here on the cruelty and harassment our daughter, Janelle, received from other girls in school, just because she was slightly different and didn't fit in. It is often said, and I believe, sadly, it is true, that women are other women's worst critics.

Another shock was waiting for me the day Lisa's mother first came to visit. Just hours before, the caseworker had called to let me know the time her mother would arrive. Just before hanging up she said, "Oh, and I thought I should let you know, Lisa's mother is a lesbian and she may be bringing her "partner" with her to see Lisa." One must remember this was happening in 1974. Many homosexuals were still "in the closet," and with my conservative, fundamental background, as far as I was concerned, they should stay there.

When "Pat" arrived, it was just as I had expected. She was a rather stocky built woman, with very short-cropped hair, dressed in slacks, a sweatshirt and loafers. Her "partner" did not come to the door, but stood at the curb, so I did not get to meet her. Pat was very cordial, introduced herself and I invited her inside. I had dressed Lisa in a very pretty, ruffled dress and had curled her long curls that by now came down to the middle of her back. She had a matching ribbon in her hair and she wore matching socks and patent leather shoes. Lisa did not run to meet her mother like so many children greet their parents after a long separation, but just very matter-of-factly walked up to her, said "Hi, mom" took her hand and they walked out the door.

To this day I still wonder how these two truck-driving, rather masculine appearing women managed to raise such a feminine, haughty-taughty little girl. Lisa was reunited with her mother a short time later and disappeared from our lives, without our ever knowing anything about her circumstances, why she was placed in foster care, or what her future would hold.

Shane

"If you just ignore it, I am sure he will stop the behavior." This was the advice given to us by the caseworker placing Shane in our care. He too arrived with his black garbage bag of possessions, however so few. He was such a tiny boy for his age. He was 5 but was much smaller than the other boys. This is a fact of many children in foster care. They are quite often much smaller than their peers. Many of them, due to neglect and lack of adequate prenatal care, are undernourished and developmentally delayed.

Shane could not look me in the eye and would lower his head whenever he was spoken to. We began a technique of taking his little chin in our hands and raising his head up when we spoke to him. We would often ask him to repeat what he said because he spoke so softly and would mumble his reply. What possibly could have happened to make this little boy so afraid to speak up?

Sexual abuse had happened... that cruel, selfish devil that robs children of their innocence and steals their childhood. This is what had happened to Shane. His mother's boyfriend had perpetrated upon him. No one will ever convince me that she was unaware of what was going on...she just didn't care. Any woman who would leave her precious child in the care of a man she had known only days could not really care about his welfare.

This selfish sick man took delight, and received sexual satisfaction, from teaching little Shane to masturbate and repeatedly demanded this of the boy. Don't get me wrong, many children, and I'm sure a very high percentage of foster children, masturbate. Many times it is their only sense of comfort and it gives them pleasure where there is no other positive stimulus available. They comfort themselves when they are left alone, abandoned and deserted, sometimes for hours on end.

That is not the case here. This was a man who was using this innocent little boy for his own selfish sexual fulfillment. As a result of the repeated demands made on him, Shane became very anxious and nervous, lost his sense of self-esteem, and he could not control his habit of masturbation. He would do it in secret, or he might do it in public. He was in a constant state of agitation. We heeded the worker's advice and would ignore the behavior most of the time. If he started in public, we would gently remove his hands and give him something to distract him. Over the next few months, with no one to stimulate this activity, and with our intervention by distracting him with another activity, it did slowly subside. He soon became busy with the normal activities a 5-year-old boy should be enjoying and he began interacting with the other children in a positive acceptable way. He learned to ride a bike, engineer an electric train and relax by being read to. It was a real sense of relief and accomplishment to see this nervous little boy, calm down, actually sleep through the night, and, yes, finally hold his head up by himself when he spoke with others.

Shane was with us for about 7 months and was returned to his mother after she agreed to have her boyfriend move out of her home. One can only wonder, without receiving counseling, if his mother's lifestyle and pattern of behavior ever changed. All we could do was provide positive intervention for him at that particular time in his young life. We have no way of knowing how this cycle of abuse would affect Shane as an adult. Without adequate counseling, there is a very good chance this sexual abuse would negatively affect him throughout his whole life.

Chris and Danny

He looked so solemn and alone. It was winter, the snow was falling and it was a cold and windy day. There was a dusting of snow on the ground and the drive to Carson City from Reno had taken me over an hour instead of the usual 30 minutes. This was my first visit to the Carson City Children's Home. Before this, I didn't even know it existed. I thought they had done away with "orphanage" type institutions years ago. Upon entering the building my first impression was how dark and bleak it seemed. The walls were a dull tan color and were noticeably void of pictures. There was minimal security. I signed in and said I was there to visit Chris. The woman at the counter pointing towards the patio door remarked "You'll find him outside on the patio." I walked over and peeked out and there he was. Chris was just 5 years old, very slight build, slightly bucked teeth, with brown hair and eyes. He was walking around in circles, then back and forth as he kicked at the snow with his sneakers. Obviously bored, he was just killing time.

It was now 1995 and we were living in Reno, Nevada. Having tired of the cold, rainy climate of Portland, we made our way to Reno, via California. I spent the last ten years working in a full time job as Administrative Assistant to the Director of Nursing at the University of Oregon Health Sciences Center, and there were no foster children in our home during those years. We worked hard, raised our two children, and were now looking forward to enjoying life in the high desert. My sister, Shirley, had moved to Reno and, with her prompting, we had checked it out and decided it would be perfect for the lifestyle we desired. We bought a 3 bedroom home and later added an additional room to accommodate a home office, and the additional children who would come to stay with us. Jay completed his education, earning a

PhD in family counseling and was happily employed as a Director of Human Resources for a local hospital.

After ten years working as an Administrative Assistant to various executives, I tired of the business world and was searching for something to do that would be more meaningful and satisfying. I was ready for a change.

While perusing the pages of the classifieds, which I often did for no particular reason, a certain ad caught my eye. It read *Foster Parents Needed.* The ad went on to describe the qualifications and the critical need for people who could care for abused and neglected children. That is it, I declared. That is what I want to do. The most fulfilling years of my life were when I was caring for the children. This definitely deserved my attention and inquiry.

What a surprise to discover the positive changes that had been instituted within the foster care system during the 10 years we were not involved. The requirements for becoming foster parents had become more stringent. There were now levels of foster care. With our educational backgrounds, the Therapeutic Foster Care level seemed the most appropriate.

Jay's degree satisfied the educational requirements and we would both attend classes to prepare us for therapeutic level foster care. The Volunteers of America was a local agency contracting with the State to provide foster care. We would apply for and become licensed therapeutic foster parents for the VOA. I would return to my "passion" and my "calling" to care for abused and neglected children.

"Hi, Chris" I said, "I'm Virginia and I'm here to visit with you." He didn't reply so I continued, "Would you mind coming inside? it's just too cold out there for me." He came in and we sat down on the well-worn, faded couch located in the big living room. "Did you get home from school early today?" I inquired. "Yeah," he replied without really looking at me. I continued, "Oh, I'm so glad they would let you out early so I could meet you. I'm sorry I'm a little late, but it's really snowing through Washoe Valley." "Oh, that's o.k." he commented, "I didn't mind waiting." The ice was broken. We were making contact. We went on to talk about his school, which he was attending temporarily since he had been brought to the Children's Home.

I asked Chris to show me around but there was not that much to see. We walked through a living room, large kitchen, long dark hallways, and bedrooms, barren, with no carpeting, walls with no pictures. He had a single bed in the corner of a large room. The blankets, obviously donated, lacked color and only added to the drab feel of the room. In his closet hung just two little shirts, a pair of jeans and there were some well-worn shoes on the floor. No toys, no books, pictures, nothing. This pierced my heart. Little boys' rooms are supposed to be red and blue and yellow with bright red fire engines on freshly painted shelves, and airplanes dangling from the ceiling. There should be piles of stuffed toys for hugging, easels for drawing and building blocks to create imaginary buildings. This room looked like something out of a 1920 Father Flannigan movie. It totally lacked of substance or personality. I decided his little boy must not be subject to these drab surroundings any longer. Chris and I visited a while and I told him it was time for me to go, but, if he agreed, I would be back soon. It amazed me at how quickly he and I had established a rapport.

On the way home, I called his caseworker on my cell phone and told her we were definitely interested in having Chris come live with us. We picked him up the next day. Two days later we were to have another big surprise.

Chris had barely unpacked his belongings, emptying out that horrid black garbage bag I came long ago to despise. Why such a big bag for just two shirts and a pair of jeans and sneakers. He acted very nonchalant about his new room, but then again, he did not want to get too excited about what might turn out to be just another temporary placement for him.

Jay had delighted in fixing up the room in a boy's motif. My sister and I shopped for "boy things" to put on the shelves and a brightly colored toy chest for treasures. We completed it with a child-sized table and chairs for arts and crafts projects and it had a special surface for building legos. My sister, Shirley, who was also my best friend, commented, "Virginia, no wonder children love coming to your house, they think they are at Disneyland!" We did manage to find Disney characters and toys to match the wallpaper and brightly colored Mickey Mouse bed spreads. We both sat on the little twin beds and content with the final result we agreed, "It will be just perfect for a little boy to enjoy."

Chris was unusually quiet and I wondered just what secrets this little boy held locked up inside of him. Something was obviously troubling him. The phone rang. "Mrs. Jeffers, this is Chris's caseworker, Mrs. Fleming from Social Services. "There is something I need to discuss with you. Is there any chance you would consider taking one more little boy? You see, Chris has a little three-year-old brother, Danny and he is also in foster care. He is with a non- English speaking family and they are really unable to care for him. We had hoped we could place him with his brother. The only concern is that he appears to be hyper- active and can be very difficult to handle." For the first time in my life I was speechless. I did not know how to answer. Another boy, hyper-active, this was certainly unexpected. "Uh, well, I'd really like to think about it. Chris is just barely getting settled in and, um, I'll have to speak with my husband about it." "I'm so sorry for springing this on you," Mrs. Fleming continued, "but the foster family just today called and asked to have Danny moved. Would you at least be willing to meet him?" "Yes, that's o.k." I agreed..." how about tomorrow?"

The visit to Danny's foster home was interesting to say the least. They were an older couple, Filipino, and spoke only a few words of English. The home was immaculate, and Danny had obviously been well taken care of; but how strange it seemed to me to have this very active little boy in a home with such elderly people who could not speak to him. When I saw that roly-poly face with those enormous, bright blue, expressive eyes, and that winning smile on his face I could not help but think he was the cutest little guy I had ever seen.

He came to me immediately and crawled up next to me on the sofa. What a little cutie I thought to myself. He does not look at all like his brother who is so somber and serious. He could not remain still and quickly slid down off the couch and began to run back and forth from his bedroom bringing me items to look at. He ran around the living room squealing with glee and then he would spin around like a top and throw himself down on the floor. What a bundle of energy I thought. That was to prove to be an understatement. Danny was the white tornado.

We arranged for a suitable car seat and agreed to take him home for a visit. I told Chris that Danny would be visiting him the next day. His little face lit up and for the first time in the two days he had been with us he cracked a smile. "Danny, Danny's comin?" "Yes", I replied and he breathed a huge sigh of relief. I did not realize at the time the burden this little boy carried for his younger brother. Their separation over the past weeks had been pure agony for him. He was to experience nightmares for several years afterwards…the same frightening dream in which he had lost Danny.

It is no wonder Chris's demeanor was so serious. He had the appearance of a premature grownup. We often said he looked and acted like a little old man. At the age of five he had shouldered the care and keeping of his three-year-old brother. When his mother, whom I will call Kelly, would be high on drugs it was Chris who, with his little brother in tow, would walk the three blocks down the busy Fourth Street corridor to the local store to buy milk and bread. It was Chris who attempted to wash the few dishes they had, in the bathtub of the Fourth street motel room they occupied. Chris had no time to be a child - he had adult responsibilities. After all, somebody had to take care of Danny.

This is where we were first introduced to the blood sucking, life destroying world of drugs and alcohol, and the long term, devastating impact they are having on the children affected in our nation. As a society we have not even begun to comprehend the tremendous cost in terms of human suffering and financial burden drugs are imposing on future generations and ours. Drug affected children born to drug addicted parents will impact our medical system and our schools in enormous proportions. To my knowledge, the cost of caring for just one drug affected child has not been fully calculated. One statistic I heard at a recent seminar, from a reliable source, stated 85% of children in foster care are there because of drug affected parents, and 85% of those parents will never recover from their drug addiction. This means the majority of the 600,000 children in foster care will never escape the system. The number of children entering the system is increasing everyday. The cost of their care is staggering.

These are a few statistics regarding Substance Abuse in this country and its impact on child abuse and neglect.

- In 2000, approximately one in four U.S. children—19 million, or 28.6% of children birth to age 17—was exposed to family alcoholism or alcohol abuse.
- Seven out of 10 cases of child abuse or neglect are exacerbated by a parent's abuse of alcohol or other drugs. In most cases, the parent's substance abuse is a long-standing problem of at least five years' duration.
- Approximately 67% of parents with children in the child welfare system require substance abuse treatment, but child welfare agencies are able to provide treatment for only 31%.
- Children whose parents abuse drugs and alcohol are almost three times more likely to be abused and four times more likely to be neglected than are children whose parents are not substance abusers.
- Children whose families do not receive appropriate treatment for alcohol and other drug abuse are more likely to end up in foster care, remain in foster care longer, and reenter once they have returned home, than are children whose families do receive treatment.
- Seventy-five percent of mothers receiving comprehensive substance abuse treatment had physical custody of one or more children six months after discharge from treatment, compared

with 54% who had custody of any children shortly before entering treatment.

In terms of human suffering, there is no way to calculate the cost of lost potential, struggle, humiliation, and hopelessness many children endure because of the effects of the drugs their parents ingested. These children, through no fault of their own, have been sentenced to a life of hardship, fraught with serious health problems, mental and physical deficiencies, and then to add insult to injury, quite often they are abandoned, left to the care of strangers.

Many ADHD children are products of drug-affected parents. Children with severe physical and mental disabilities are often the result of strokes in utero sustained by drug-affected mothers during their pregnancies. The two children currently in our care, you will learn more about in detail later in this book, are both children who suffered strokes before they were born. Subsequently, they suffer from mental retardation, cerebral palsy, and are legally blind. Their mothers used drugs while pregnant. On an even sadder note, many children who are not rescued and remain with their drug-addicted parents never receive the care they require. The parents use the children's disability funds to purchase drugs to feed their habits. Even though the government provides free medical care for these children, their drug-affected parents are not capable of following through with obtaining the necessary services, nor do they follow through with the required medical treatment for their children.

If people were aware of the financial burden the care of these innocent human beings is imposing on society, perhaps there would be an outcry. Even more, why is there no outcry to stop the suffering incurred by innocent children every day because of drugs and alcohol. Where are the champions of the cause for the children? It seems to me, there are more outcries over the abuse of animals and the pillage of the environment than there are over the abuse and destruction of innocent children through the infiltration, acceptance and even glamorization of drug use in our society.

It is very difficult for me to watch a TV comedian or a popular TV sitcom make light of the use of drugs when I live with their devastating effects every day as I care for my two developmentally delayed and physically disabled foster children. Their lives have been just as devastated by pot, cocaine, alcohol and heroin as if they had been shot. Still we continue to laugh at, look the other way and, at times, even glamorize the use of drugs and alcohol, as if we were in total denial of the devastation is has brought upon innocent children.

Getting to know Danny taught us what ADHD is, in the truest sense of the word. Danny was a bundle of energy who was in constant motion. Chris also suffered from attention deficit hyper activity disorder, which made it difficult for him to concentrate on a subject for any length of time, and to stay focused on a project was nearly impossible.

Chris turned 6 shortly after he came to us and Danny turned 4 a couple of months later. The boys were obviously thrilled and happy to be together again. They enjoyed sharing their new room and we soon learned sending them to their room was not considered by them to be punishment. When a child has lived in a succession of motel rooms, without his own room to retreat to, having his own space offered him freedom and privacy he had not experienced before. The boys loved their room and completely enjoyed everything in it. Chris loved to read and learn about dinosaurs and other creatures. Danny loved to build legos and make things with his building blocks. They both seemed to adjust well to their new living accommodations.

Once the boys were comfortable with us they began to ask questions about their mother "Kelly." They wanted to know her whereabouts and if she was ok. I find it interesting many foster children call their parents by their first names, instead of mommy and daddy. I don't know of any particular reason for this and I don't render any significance to it, but it did strike me as rather odd. However, most of them would immediately ask if they could call us Mom and Dad. We agreed. I believe children need a "mommy" and I explained to them a "mommy" is someone who loves and cares for a child. This explanation always seemed to suffice. Now, as we are older, sometimes it feels strange to me, when I am old enough to be their grandmother, to have these little kids calling me "mommy." I used to be concerned about what people might think but I finally outgrew that concern. If these little ones need to call someone Mommy then it's all right with me. We do get some odd looks from strangers though.

Connie, the children's caseworker did share with us the boys' history, which prepared us to deal with their many problems in an educated manner. Kelly and the boys' father, Mike, had been married. They both became addicted to drugs before the boys were born. Sustaining their habits drained them of all of their financial resources. We learned on more than one occasion the boys' grandmother, Carol, had bailed her daughter out and helped her financially. Twice she had secured an apartment for her daughter's family, purchased furniture, paid utilities, and helped Kelly and Mike get a fresh start.

On both occasions, within two months Kelly and Mike failed to pay their rent, pawned the furniture and even sold their children's toys and clothes to pay for their narcotics. They were then forced to move into a cheap motel with the children. We were surprised as we drove through the low-rent district, the Fourth Street corridor of Reno. The boys announced as we passed various run-down motels, "Oh we lived there" or "That's where Kelly lives." They had experienced drifting from one dirty motel to another, quite often being forced to leave their belongings behind.

The pawn shops of Reno are further testimony of the desperation of people to secure money to purchase their daily "fix." Many caring and loving parents and grandparents, just like Carol, try to help their drug addicted children, if for no other reason than the grandchildren. They buy nice gifts for their grandchildren only to have these items pawned for a small percentage of their value - not to buy groceries or pay utilities, but to buy drugs. I recently purchased a Nintendo game from a pawnshop for our children. I asked the pawnbroker why they had so many newer games available. His response was, "Oh, the first thing people pawn when they need money is their children's toys." It is sad to consider, but many of the toys provided to the underprivileged at Christmas, or purchased and wrapped with the hands of loving grandparents, aunts and uncles, are quite often sitting in the pawnbroker's windows before New Year's Day.

The boy's grandmother, Carol was struggling on her own at this time. Her only daughter, Kelly, had been adopted as a small child. Carol loved her as her own and I am sure never anticipated the devastation and heartbreak her daughter's addiction would cause. Carol loved her two little grandsons and it broke her heart to see them with their lives in a constant state of disruption. Carol lived in California but would make the long four-hour drive each weekend to visit the boys. By now they had been picked up by the authorities suffering from neglect and were being integrated into the foster care system. Carol was determined not to lose these boys. She fervently hoped, miraculously, her daughter would overcome her addiction and become a responsible mother. However, time would soon run out.

Recently enacted Federal statutes require that long range planning for each child in foster care be put in place. Social Workers have been given the mandate to have a permanency plan in place for each child within one year. Parents now are given 18 months to "get their act together'" or face termination of their parental rights. Even with these laws in place, however, some children still remain in the system, with no permanent placement long after the 18 months have run out.

With social services overworked and understaffed, it is difficult to police each case to its conclusion. Many parents have learned how to "work the system." They will move out of state and request an ICPC and their case is transferred to a new caseworker who, unfamiliar with the case, will have to begin the cycle all over.

We were also introduced to a wonderful organization at this time, *CASA*. This is a group of volunteers who become *Court Appointed Special Advocates* and these wonderful people advocate for foster children. Unfortunately, there are not enough of these volunteers to go around. Our boys, however, did have a wonderful CASA worker, Marge, who was to follow their case from the beginning to its conclusion. She was there for these boys, tirelessly working to make sure their case was followed, and decisions made in their best interests. Marge was aware of how manipulative Kelly could be and how, through a various succession of caseworkers, she was able on two occasions to get her children back. Marge, with the court's permission, followed up with them, and when Kelly returned to her old habits and began neglecting the boys, Marge was able to report this to the court. After investigation the boys were again removed from Kelly. Marge kept accurate and detailed records of every incident. This way, when a new caseworker was assigned to the case, or they faced a different judge, Kelly was not able to manipulate her way through the system. Marge was there to provide the history of the boys repeated neglect and the mother's repeated failure to comply with the court orders regarding the care of her children.

Marge also provided stability in these boys' lives over a three-year period. She would pick them up and take them for outings. She bought them clothing and books and toys. She took them to her home to swim in her swimming pool. She was not only an advocate, but also a friend to these two little guys. She grew to love and care for them. After they came to live with us and she saw the stability in their lives, she did begin to relax a little. She then had time to devote to other cases she was assigned.

Marge shared with me her concern the boys' grandmother, Carol, was beginning to ask questions about gaining custody of her grandsons. Marge expressed to me her worry was that the grandmother was only seeking custody in order to be able to turn the boys back over to their mother. This was a possibility but later was proven not to be the case. In any event, not enough can be said about the wonderful volunteers of CASA who so unselfishly give of themselves to advocate for foster children. They are quite often unseen heroes, making a radical difference in the life of a small child.

Living with two hyperactive boys in the house was no small task. Their inability to keep their attention on any one activity for any length of time was exhausting. Danny was like a spinning top. He would move from one toy or game to another, one room to another, without stopping. It seemed he had an unusual amount of energy and stamina. We'll never forget the first time, about a week after the boys had been reunited and were living together with us, they literally tore their room apart. It had been about an hour since we looked in on them when I heard a loud crash and quickly ran to their room. It looked like a bomb had exploded. They had thrown everything everywhere. The shelves were bare and some of them hanging by a screw. Pictures were lopsided, and their bedding was ripped from their beds. When I lost my cool and yelled "What happened in here?" They both just looked at me in astonishment... "Oh, we were just playing." I learned the hard way they could not be left alone, nor could their bedroom door be closed for any length of time. They were acting out like little wild men. Danny, when disciplined, would scream at the top of his lungs and could hold out for hours. Chris would become angry and sullen. He resorted to kicking the walls and would bang his head against the wall if put in "time out," It didn't take a rocket scientist to see that these two little boys were totally "out of control." I now understood why they had previously been placed in separate homes. They played off of each other and egged each other on. They were used to, and seemed to enjoy, creating chaos.

In the beginning a trip in the car was also a nightmare. They could not sit still. Danny was confined to a car seat which helped somewhat, but they still managed to wiggle, kick, wrestle and hit. Finally, in desperation, on one outing when they were getting out of hand I warned them, "If you don't settle down, I am turning the car around and taking you home." They continued with their tousling. I abruptly stopped the car, turned it around and drove home. The look of surprise on their faces was unforgettable. Danny's big blue eyes were the size of silver dollars. Chris began to cry when he realized the trip to the Dairy Queen had just been axed. They began to beg and promise to behave but I would not be swayed. We parked the car. I marched them both directly up to their room and declared "No more trips until you can settle down in the car." I wish I could say that was the end of it... it wasn't. It took at least two more such "turn around and go home" incidents before they figured out we meant business. These boys certainly knew how to "push the envelope."

We also learned to "divide and conquer" with the boys and this did make our lives easier. On various outings I would take one boy one time and the other the next. This only works, of course, if you have sufficient help and someone to watch one child at home while the other gets to go.

Our first trips to the department store were equally disastrous. Danny would sit in the shopping cart and grab for everything within his reach. He grabbed items off the shelves and got into items that were already in the cart. I really had my hands full. Once I made the mistake of letting him out of the cart and he and Chris ran wildly through the clothing racks, knocking down displays, screaming at each other and hiding from me. I was exhausted by the end of the trip and vowed never again to put myself through such an ordeal.

Such is the life of a mother with two hyperactive children. Believe me, it is no picnic. This experience has also made me more tolerant when I see young mothers dealing with obviously hyperactive children. I used to raise my eyebrows in disapproval of such an unruly child; now I am much more patient and compassionate. Not ALL children who are demanding and unruly are just spoiled and undisciplined.... in some cases these are children who are unable to control their behavior and in need of medical and or psychological intervention.

This raises the question regarding Ritalin. There has been so much controversy regarding the administration of this drug to children. The pendulum seems to have swung from one extreme to the other regarding opinions on the use of this drug. There has been an outcry over the seeming over dispensing of this drug used to slow down hyperactive children. Statistics are quoted and misquoted regarding how many children in a given classroom may be taking this medication. I, for one, am not amazed at the increasing amount of children requiring this intervention. When you consider the increased popularity of drug use in this country, the subsequent increase in children adversely affected by prenatal exposure to drugs, and the ultimate outcome resulting in a hyperactive child, we should not be shocked that we are producing more children with ADHD. I am more concerned with the incorrect diagnosis of ADHD than with the prescribing of Ritalin for a child who is accurately diagnosed with this disorder.

We witnessed first hand the difference Ritalin can make in the child who is truly ADHD. Chris was diagnosed as ADHD and prescribed Ritalin. The transformation was dramatic and almost immediate. He was able to gain control of his actions, slow down, and began to function normally. He was no longer disruptive in class and consequently his classmates began to associate with him. His self-esteem improved and he began to succeed in his schoolwork. He was finally able concentrate and focus.

I learned there are two theories about how Ritalin works. The most popular is Ritalin slows down a child's nervous system resulting in his decreased activity level. The other, which was shared with me by a well know pediatrician, and makes sense to me, is Ritalin actually speeds up a child's nervous system. The child is actually underactive and slow, and his constant movements are a result of his attempt to stimulate himself. Once he receives Ritalin, it speeds up his brain activity so he doesn't have to constantly be in motion to keep himself stimulated. He is then able to calm down and is able to concentrate. We know Ritalin acts like a stimulant when given to adults and so how the theory that it acts the opposite in children was developed is a bit mystifying to me. This is why I believe in the latter theory, but readily admit I am not a scientist and claim no expertise, other than experience, regarding the subject. I just know first hand what a dramatic change we saw in our two boys with proper medical intervention.

In Chris's and Danny's case, Ritalin was a lifesaver. The boys were impossible to live with and to control until they were diagnosed with ADHD and treatment was initiated. They continued with the medicine and both of them dramatically improved in school, at home and socially.

Many foster children are not only deprived physically, but often culturally. We have fostered children in our home who had never visited a park, a zoo, seen the ocean, or been on an extended vacation. Their lives were just merely an existence, surviving from day to day. Their parents lived from fix-to-fix, and the children were just "there." Also, there are some families who may, through no fault of their own, live in abject poverty. They are consumed with the day-to-day struggle for survival. They literally live from hand to mouth and are concerned with where the next meal is coming from. This leaves no room or time to enjoy and experience the true wonders of the world around them. I was absolutely appalled, and deeply saddened, when I discovered one of our little children had never even been taken to a park. His entire existence had been confined to a two-room apartment. No one ever took the time to let him feed the ducks or feel the cool breeze brush against his face from atop a swing. He did not know the simple joy of a merry-go-round or a teeter-totter. He had spent his first 4 years either propped in front of a TV set or left to entertain himself with a few broken infant toys.

One of the joys of foster parenting is seeing the delight in a child's eyes when he is introduced to new places and experiences. This was to be one of many pleasures with Chris and Danny. There are many television ads that show the adventures and excitement Disneyland has to offer. If these ads are meant to entice children to beg their parents for a trip to Disneyland, they certainly succeed. The boys would often see these commercials and talk among themselves about how wonderful it would be to visit Disneyland. We, too, began to dream about a vacation to the magical kingdom. It had been years since we had been there. We had taken Brent and Janelle when they were 6 and 2, and I still had an imprint in my mind of their excitement at visiting this children's wonderland. We would occasionally drag out the photos and reminisce about the wonderful times we had enjoyed.

How could we provide such an experience for Chris and Danny? Once the idea was hatched in my mind, it soon became on obsession. There had to be a way. Over the next few months we began saving every dollar we could in hopes of making the dream a reality for the boys. We didn't dare mention it to them because it would be just too disappointing if, for some reason, we were unable to make it happen.

My sister-in-law, Jeannie who lives in Orlando, Florida, was working for Walt Disney World. I mentioned to her how we would like to take the boys on a "dream vacation." We had just about enough saved for the motel and the airfare from Reno to Orange County, and now we just needed enough for the admission. Jeannie informed me that if I would write to the Public Relations Department of Disneyland, explaining our situation, there was a slight chance we might be able to obtain complimentary passes. The possibility was so exciting, and so immediately I wrote them, telling them of Chris and Danny and our desire to show them Disneyland. I sincerely prayed over that letter and dropped it in the mail never really expecting to receive a response.

You can imagine my elation, when, just two weeks later I received a letter from the wonderful staff at Disneyland saying they would provide admission, not only for the boys, but for the four of us to visit the Magic Kingdom! This was a dream come true.

I became so excited that I decided to write to Knott's Berry Farm and within another week we received admission passes to their amusement park as well. I never cease to be amazed at the generosity of others, and giving hearts there are in this country. We are the most generous, caring nation in the world. We delight in assisting and lifting the burdens of the less fortunate. Many have truly found the true joy of giving and we ascribe to the "better to give than to receive" truth in our lives.

We waited until the last minute to tell the boys we were taking them to Disneyland. I believe their little nervous systems just could not have handled it any sooner than necessary. Of course there was permission to be obtained, and papers to take them out of the State to be approved; but at last, we were on our way to Disneyland.

Just going to the airport and boarding the plane was thrilling to the boys. Neither had ever flown before. I pity the poor souls who had to sit in the seats in front of and behind us. Even with medication to calm them down Chris and Danny were wound tighter than drums. They both giggled with glee and had a hundred questions to ask. Danny had to twist every knob, fasten and unfasten his seat belt, climb over Jay to see out the window and announce to everyone around us that he was going to the Magic Kingdom.

We managed to secure a window seat for each boy and, amazingly, once the airplane took off, they were both so mesmerized by what they saw as they peered out the tiny windows, they actually calmed down and enjoyed the flight.

We had a smooth flight and Jay secured a rental car we drove to our motel. For the economy rates I had managed to secure, the motel really was quite nice, complete with swimming pool and sauna. We had two king-sized beds, a TV and a little refrigerator. We unpacked, and since it was midday, very hot and humid outside, we decided to take the boys for a swim. This cool retreat, however, needed to be postponed temporarily.

From the moment we arrived at the motel Chris seemed a little edgy. He checked and rechecked the refrigerator. "There's no food in here," he exclaimed. "Oh, that's o.k. Chris," Jay replied, "Well pick up a few things later." But Chris was not satisfied. Again he opened the little door of the miniature refrigerator, "Dad, we really need to get some food!" "Later, Chris," said Jay, "C'mon, let's go check out the pool." Chris did not budge. "Please, dad, can't we just go get some milk and bread? I don't want Danny to get hungry."

All of a sudden it hit us like a ton of bricks. Chris had spent most of his few years living in and out of cheap motels. To him, this was just another move. He thought we were going to live here. He reverted back to the survival mode and his greatest concern was that his younger brother not go hungry. We sat both of the boys down and explained to them that we were on vacation. We would be staying at the motel while we visited Disneyland and then we would be returning to Reno. Chris remained skeptical and we could tell he was very unsure of the situation. He was not convinced this was not just another home. Sensing his insecurity, and with the understanding and compassion of the loving father he is, Jay took Chris by the hand and said "Come on, Chris, I'm sure there's a grocery store nearby where we can get some groceries." They were gone about twenty minutes and returned with enough food to fill the little refrigerator. They bought milk, bread, peanut butter, jam, cookies and some apples. Jay let Chris put the items in the refrigerator. Once this was finished and Chris seemed satisfied knowing there were ample provisions, we all got into our bathing suits and went out to cool down in the swimming pool.

This incident is a constant reminder to me of how much we all take for granted and how little we know about those living in poverty. There are families literally living from meal to meal and when there is no food available they just go without. This is what our two little boys had been through, countless times, since infancy.

We also realized the boys did not understand what a vacation was. Even after we told them we were going to Disneyland for a vacation the fact we had packed suitcases and gone to a motel signaled to them we had moved. They had done this so many times in their young lives they thought this was just another move. We sat them down and explained once again this is what people do; they take vacations, go to a motel and then visit wonderful places. Innocently, once again four-year-old Danny looked up and said "Dad, how long are we going to live here, we forgot to pack my other toys?"

We enjoyed a wonderful dinner out and then settled back in our motel for the evening. The boys were so wound up we didn't think we would ever get them to settle down. Finally, we got them tucked in and they fell asleep, knowing tomorrow would be the big day.

We woke early the next morning as expected with two very excited little boys. No coaching needed this morning to get them dressed, groomed and ready to go. They jabbered all through breakfast and convinced us not to wait for our second cup of coffee. They were ready to get going.

The look on Chris and Danny's little faces when they saw the entrance to Disneyland was one of shear astonishment. I'm sure they never imagined it was so much larger than life. The music playing, the other children pulling their parents excitedly towards the ticket lines, one could just feel the momentum building. It was almost too much excitement for two little boys to handle. At last we were inside and there it all was before us...just like in the TV advertisements. Then came the moment I will never forget as long as I live. Precious little Danny looked up at me with that moon face of his and those huge round, deep blue eyes and said with his little lisp, "Mommy, am I dweaming or am I weally at Disneywand?"

Over the years so many people have asked us "Why do you do this?" And now, "At your age, you should be free from children, and enjoying retirement." I tell them, "Unless you could have been there and seen the look in little Danny's eyes, that angelic face, and heard that sweet pleading as he wondered out loud if something so wonderful was really happening to him, or if he was just dreaming it, you may never understand why we would find such enjoyment and satisfaction in foster care."

We believe every child deserves a childhood, but we also know the reality some of them are robbed of this wonderful time of innocence and discovery. While some children are riding the merry-go-round and roller coasters of life, there are little ones, huddled in a corner, shivering in the cold, alone, wondering where their next meal is coming from.

Granted, many of these children are returned to the deprived situations from which they came, but somehow, if we can just give them a glimpse of how wonderful the world can be, perhaps this will stimulate them to rise above their circumstances and seek a better life as they mature. Perhaps some lingering memory of Disneyland will prompt them to realize that there is a more fulfilling existence and give them hope that someday it will be theirs.

Chris and Danny's mother, Kelly, sought custody of the boys through the court system. However, she was never able to stay clean and sober long enough to even attend all of her court hearings. One custody hearing we attended for the boys Kelly even showed up high on marijuana. The judge ordered her handcuffed, removed from the courtroom and taken to jail. There was just no way this young woman was ever going to get her life together and be able to care for her children. She could not hold a job or keep an apartment. Her money was being sucked up by her drug addiction.

The year we had the boys God was working a wonderful miracle for their grandmother, Carol. We always knew that God would not abandon these boys. He had a plan for their lives. It was our job just to wait and see what that plan would be. As it turned out, over the next twelve months Carol was to meet a wonderful man, David, a divorced father of two grown boys. He and Carol were soon married, found a church to attend and soon the two of them were making the trip over the mountain each weekend to see the boys.

Jay and I really liked David and Carol and had such a good feeling about them. We could tell they were "solid" people and soon our instincts proved to be true. They shared with us their desire to adopt Chris and Danny and give them the permanent home they deserved.

We also related to them our decision that if, for some reason, the right family was not found for the boys, we had decided we would adopt them ourselves. We made this decision with fear and trepidation, knowing the huge responsibility this posed, at our age, to raise two ADHD little boys. It seemed overwhelming but we believed, if this were to be our task, God would give us the strength and grace to carry it through. Ultimately, He chose not to require this of us. Needless to say we were both very grateful and relieved to find out Carol and David were willing to fight to gain custody of Carol's grandsons. They would one day go home to their "real" family.

DCFS and the courts really put Carol and David through the ringer. They had to jump through hoops, dot every "I" and cross every "T". On a positive note, DCFS required Carol and David to seek counseling for themselves and the boys. They needed to learn all that was available about ADHD. Carol shared with me after the boys were returned to her how appreciative she was of the counseling they received and of the time we spent with them, sharing what we knew about the disorder, and how we dealt with Chris and Danny. Unfortunately, many well meaning people think, "love will take care of everything," but this is just not true when it comes to living with a hyperactive child. One must gain knowledge and be given the tools necessary in dealing with the day-to-day crises involved in caring for a child with ADHD.

Knowing her mother was adopting Chris and Danny, Kelly would quickly relinquish her parental rights. This saved the courts and DCFS considerable time and money involved in such a legal action. Sometimes this process can take months and even years to accomplish. The courts seem to bend over backwards in favor of the biological mother giving her every opportunity, time and time again, to get her act together and show she can provide adequately for her children. The requirements are minimal, and yet many of these parents cannot even provide the minimum required: hold down a job, provide a place to live, obtain childcare if the mother is away from the home working, and remain clean and sober.

We've witnessed the agencies working with the mothers, helping them find work, getting them situated in an apartment, and finding childcare. The children are returned to the parents and then bang, within just days or weeks the mother loses her job because she fails to show up or she does not have adequate transportation. She may have a new boyfriend move in and he begins using up her financial resources. She fails to take the children to school and soon she uses her welfare subsidy for drugs and booze.

In Reno, many parents will leave small children in their apartment homes, at night, alone for hours, and go to the casinos to gamble away their paychecks or welfare checks.

It is also no surprise at how quickly, once the children are removed from the home, the mother's "boyfriend" disappears from the scene. Once he knows the welfare money for the children will no longer be coming in, the well has gone dry, he moves on to greener pastures. The mother is then left without her children, her boyfriend, or welfare support. If she has been drug addicted she quickly turns to her only comfort, her drugs or alcohol. Often she will wind up in jail for possession, loses her job, and winds up back on the street. The children begin another cycle within the system and in another foster home. Depending on where the foster home is located, this can once again mean adjusting to a new home, a possible change in schools, and leaving their friends, to again be strangers in a new home, new school, and new neighborhood.

Watching Carol and David pack up the car with the boys' things was truly a time of mixed emotions. We were happy and relieved to know these two little guys we had come to love so deeply would be going to a permanent, Christian home with two people who loved them so much. Yet we knew there would be emptiness in our hearts and home that is hard to describe. We would miss the sound of their laughter, all those hugs and high fives, reading them bedtime stories and tucking them in. They had become such a delight in our lives. Chris's sincere caring for others and Danny's giggles, big blue eyes and infectious smile brought so much joy and laughter into our home. Now all of that would be gone.

We realized that this was the final outcome we hoped and prayed for in each of our foster children's lives. This would be a "success story," and a positive outcome for these little boys who had spent so much time in foster care. They were the lucky ones. Most stories do not have such a good outcome. This was how foster care should work: Children taken from an unsafe, unstable environment, placed with loving, caring foster parents who could nurture them and provide an environment where they could heal from their wounds, be given proper care and therapy, and then ultimately, placed with a permanent family, hopefully from among their natural family members, and given a chance at some normalcy in their young lives. This time the system had worked.

We have kept in touch with Carol and David the past ten years and the boys are doing as well as can be expected given the trauma in their young lives. At this writing, Danny is blossoming, does well in school and is a happy boy. Chris, on the other hand, has had some serious problems. He is dealing with his anger and often strikes out angrily at school and at home. He does not do as well in school and the struggle to learn is sometimes overwhelming for him. He remains in counseling to deal with his deep seated anger. Carol and David express their concern for him and are seeking every available resource to help him deal with his emotions. His future success is "guarded" at this time. We can only pray he can overcome his feelings of abandonment, loss of childhood and anger towards the world that, understandably, he feels has not treated him fairly. It will take a lifetime of healing for this young man….When hurts are so deep, for such an extended period of time, sometimes it takes a miracle. This is what we pray for Chris.

Regarding family relationships and children in foster care, it is well known close, nurturing relationships with parents, kin, and other caregivers allow and encourage children and young people to grow and thrive. Caring relationships with community members strengthen social and relationship skills, improve self-mastery, and enhance self-esteem.

Statistics from the *National Fact Sheet* indicate:

- Of the 542,000 children in foster care in 2012, approximately 24% lived with relatives while in care. Of the children 26,084 exiting foster care that year, 10% Nearly 11,670 adopted children (23%) were adopted by relatives.

- In 2012, 405,000 children lived in some form of court-involved relative or kinship care; more than half lived in families with incomes below 200% of the federal poverty level.

- In 2012, 2.2 million children lived in relatives' homes, without their parents, in kinship care. Grandparents cared for almost 57% of these children; an aunt or uncle cared for 22%.

- Teenagers represent the largest proportion of children in kinship care (44%). Forty-four percent of youth in kinship care are black non-Hispanic, 38% are white non-Hispanic, 15% are Hispanic, and 3% are of another race or ethnicity.

- More than 1 million parents were incarcerated in prisons or local jails in 2010, affecting 2.3 million children

Jose & Angelina

After the departure of Chris and Danny we took a year off from foster care to catch our breath. We sold our two-story home in favor of a single level home on the other side of Reno in a burgeoning new community called Sparks. Looking towards retirement this home was much more suited for our needs.

One day while perusing the newspaper classifieds, as I often do just for fun... a particular ad caught my eyes. "Foster parents needed for Level II and Therapeutic care for special needs children. Call Koinonia Foster Homes at this number". More out of curiosity than anything else I found myself dialing the number. I was curious as to who this agency was and what their program was. This one phone call was to bring a whole new dimension of foster care into our lives – caring for developmentally and physically challenged children.

Koinonia is a not-for-profit, private agency that contracts with the State to provide homes for foster children. Many state agencies, we were to discover, are turning to private agencies to meet the ever growing need for foster homes. Working with this agency has been an enormous help to us as foster parents. Their caseworkers carry a smaller caseload compared to State social workers. Thus we have much greater support and available resources. This agency also makes available the training classes we need to obtain and maintain our Therapeutic or Treatment Group Home, license status. Over the last 20 years we have worked with this private agency and it has truly made our work as foster parents more manageable. We have come to appreciate some wonderful, professional, sincere people through the private agency.

Although they were not developmentally or physically challenged, little 4-year-old Jose' and his 3 year old sister, Angelina, were emotionally challenged. They both suffered from severe neglect and possible sexual abuse. These two were possibly the most beautiful children we had ever seen or taken care of in our home. Both children were the product of a Caucasian mother and alien Hispanic fathers. With their beautiful black wavy hair, compelling pitch black eyes, and tan skin, they were both just too adorable for words.

Once again there is a similar scenario. Mother goes to work and leaves her small children alone in a run down apartment with their nine-year-old brother in charge. Their older brother, Armando, who had been sexually abused by one of the men who came through the revolving door of his mother's apartment, had himself attempted to sexually abuse his younger brother, Jose'. We were to suspect later Angelina too had been sexually abused, but we are not sure by whom. On one occasion we were to find little five-year-old Jose' attempting to be sexual with her.

The children arrived at our home with practically no clothing and very few toys or personal possession. Angelina especially looked so unkempt. Her hair was in tangles and her clothes did not fit. Jose' just needed a bath and a haircut and some clean clothes.

Our daughter Janelle, who helps us with the children, takes personal delight in taking the new little ones shopping and outfitting them with new clothes. She loves seeing just how cute she can dress them and fix their hair. It is also amazing what it does for a little child's self-esteem to have new clothes, shoes and an appropriate hair style.

Janelle's first assignment, much to her delight, was a trip to Penny's, Mervyns and Walmart for new duds for the kids. They needed everything from new underwear and socks to shoes, dresses for Angelina, jeans and shirts for Jose'. A new jacket topped off the list. Then it was over to Walmart for ribbons and scrunchies for Angelina's beautiful long hair. She was especially pleased to pick out a little purse with a matching wallet inside. Each child selected a new comb and brush and toiletries. Angelina squealed with delight as she selected a perfumed body splash. Jose' selected a Toy Story towel and matching washcloth and toothbrush.

What excitement as all of the new items were put carefully away in their proper places. Each child had a bathroom drawer of their own, a section in the closet of their own, as well as two dresser drawers for his clothing. It was amazing to me how quickly these two children adjusted to their new surroundings. This just proved once again to me the resiliency of children. One might expect a child to cry his first night in a strange place, and certainly we have had children who did just that, but these two were just too exhausted, and they each fell right asleep after they were tucked into their little beds.

10:30 p.m. is about the time we usually retire, after the late evening news. We always check in on the children before retiring and this night was no different. You can imagine my surprise when going into the bedroom and seeing Jose' sound asleep in his bed but Angelina was not in her little toddler bed. I looked around the room, then in the bathroom thinking she might have had to get up in the night, but she was not there. Quickly I turned on the night-light and began a more thorough check of her bedroom.... And then I found her. She was huddled up with her blanket, under her bed as close to the wall as she could get.... and as far from the reach of anyone looking for her as possible. She was sound asleep. I called for Jay, and he carefully moved the bed so we could get her and put her in her little bed. She moaned softly, then turned over and went back to sleep. This was not to be the last such incident. We would find her "hiding" in the closet underneath her blanket... as far in a corner as she could get. It soon became obvious to us something had happened to this little girl that made her afraid to sleep in her own bed. After sharing our suspicions with the therapist it was concluded she probably had been taken from her bed in the night and molested. What heartbreak to think of the fear that drove her to "hide" at night. A child's room and little bed should be a place of warmth and safety and peace... hers had been a place of abuse and fear.

Endeavoring not to change Angelina's routine too much, I began taking her to the daycare/preschool center where her mother had taken her on occasion. She seemed to enjoy going there and was not the least bit timid when I dropped her off. About three weeks after beginning this routine the daycare supervisor asked if she could speak to me. I agreed. She told me, "We cannot believe the change in Angelina in the last three weeks. When her mother used to drop her off she was hungry, dirty, and her hair was matted. She would go and sit in a corner by herself and rock back and forth. She would not join in with the other children and when we tried to get close to her she would have a tantrum and scream "Leave me alone, don't touch me!" She continued, "Now she comes in and the first thing she does is show off her new clothes. We can't help but compliment her on how adorable she looks and how pretty her hair is. She then twirls around and giggles with glee. She is now joining in with the other children and she is just so happy!! I just thought you would want to know what a difference we have all seen in her and how very pleased we are for her."

Upon inquiry, the supervisor told me of her interactions with Angelina's mother. "The woman was so rude and crude. On a couple of occasions I had to ask her to leave because she was using foul language, swearing at Angelina, and we couldn't permit it around the other children." She continued, "On one occasion I had to threaten to call the police if she did not leave the premises. Yet, she kept coming back and dropping Angelina off." This was probably because this was a State subsidized program and they are in short supply. She commented "I would liked to have told her not to come back anymore but I just felt so sorry for Angelina I didn't have the heart to do it."

Jose' was such a handsome little guy. He was short and stocky and very strong. He spoke with a lisp and we had him enrolled in speech therapy in a Head Start program. Eventually we had both of the children enrolled in Head Start with hopes of improving their social skills and interaction with their peers. We were to discover very quickly Jose' had a very bad temper and would react in rage if anyone invaded his territory or personal space. At Head Start he would not hesitate to punch another child if he wanted a certain toy or to be first in line. When his actions required a "time out" he would refuse and when separated from the others and put in a "time out" area he would begin to scream at the top of his lungs...and we found out he could keep this up for an hour or longer. We have a well-lit laundry room at the end of our hallway that has become our time out place. On many occasions we would sit Jose' on the rug in the laundry room with the door open so he could calm down. On several occasions he managed to scream and kick and carry on for what seemed like hours. Eventually he would wear himself out or realize no one was listening to him and calm down. We would keep checking on him and asking him if he was ready to return to the rest of the family. Finally, sometimes exhausted, he would say, "Yes, I ready now," and come out of time out and be very peaceful and calm. We figured this little boy was just so full of rage and anger he needed to get it all out. These episodes became fewer and farther between as time went on.

It should be noted we do not punish children because they are expressing their anger. Most of these children have a good reason and a right to be angry. We just want to ensure they do not harm themselves or others when they are releasing this anger, either through a tantrum, flailing about, or screaming. We just give them a place to do this, in our case the laundry room.

On the other hand, Jose' also had this very sweet, loving side to him. Quite often he would come and lie on the couch and put his head on my lap and just want to talk to me, or ask me to sing to him. I would rub his little head and tell him stories or sing little children's songs to him. I could feel the tension going out of him. Sometimes I made up little songs with his name in them and this particularly delighted him. I'd sing songs like "Jesus loves Jose' this I know, for the Bible tells me so. Little ones like Jose' to him belong, Jose' is weak, but He is strong. Yes, Jesus loves Jose', Yes, Jesus loves Jose', Yes, Jesus loves Jose', the Bible tells me so." He would giggle delightedly and ask me to repeat the songs over and over. These were very special times for both of us.

Another very important thing we have always done with the children in our care is to pray over them. As little Jose' lay there with his head on my lap, relaxed, feeling safe and secure, I would lay my hands on his chest or his forehead. Silently, I would pray for him, "Please, Lord, heal this little boy's emotions and remove the emotional scars he has. Please erase the bad memories and replace them with new, happy ones. Let him know, Lord, just how much you love and care for him, and you have a wonderful plan for his life. Help us to show him that there are good people in the world who love and care for others, and his life can be worthwhile and without violence. Help us to show him just how special and wonderful he is."

Jose' and Angelina were to stay with us for just a little over a year. During that time their mother, Tracy, never gave up trying to get them back. I attended a couple of hearings including one involving the State's intent to terminate her parental rights. Tracy was instructed to attend parenting classes, get a job, and show she could provide a home for her children. She never complied with one thing the court or DCFS asked of her. She would get a job but then lose it within a matter of weeks. She always had an excuse, "The supervisor doesn't like me" or "I couldn't find a baby sitter," or "My car broke down," etc. The same went for her counseling. Not one counselor provided for her by the State met with her approval. Of course anytime they suggested a change in her lifestyle so she could care for her children she resented being told what to do. She never followed through with the counseling or the parenting classes. Without a job it was impossible for her to find a decent place to live. When she did get an apartment, within a short period of time she had a new boyfriend move in with her. Again she would leave her children in the care of her boyfriend while she made a feeble attempt to get a job.

The last court hearing I attended involving Tracy she did not attend. She phoned in instead claiming she couldn't make it to the hearing. Another indication the State bends over backwards to accommodate the biological parents in hopes of keeping families together. When the Judge asked her why the State should not terminate her rights Tracy had only excuses for her not meeting the requirements. Then the Judge opened it up for anyone in the courtroom to speak up. I could not resist. "Your Honor" I said. "I am the foster mother for Jose and Angelina and they have been in my home for over a year now. In that time the ONLY thing their mother Tracy has done, to my knowledge, is to have another baby." Yes, this was the case. With no job, not attending parenting classes, a meager apartment to live in, Tracy had just had her fourth baby, by a fourth illegal alien, who, like the other three fathers of her children, was not paying any child support. At this hearing the Judge declared the State would proceed with terminating her parental rights.

Termination of Tracy's parental rights was never to happen. Tracy knew how to play the system. As a second-generation welfare recipient, her mother having raised three children while on welfare, Tracy knew how to get around the court system and DCFS. She knew if she waited long enough eventually a new social worker would be appointed to her case and she could "bluff" the new caseworker. This is exactly what happened. So, following the hearing, Tracy moved to Ohio with her sister, rented a mobile home and then requested an ICPC to have her children's case transferred to Ohio. The State of Nevada easily complied and the children were removed from our home and sent to Ohio to become a part of the Ohio foster care system. With a new caseworker, a new state, and without ever complying with one requirement set forth by the state to enable her to get her children back, Tracy regained custody of her children in the State of Ohio. Less than six months after regaining custody of her children in Ohio, Tracy, along with her four children, moved back to Nevada.

I am sad to say I can't even imagine what is happening with those children today. Janelle did run into the children and their grandmother one afternoon outside of the movie theatre. Angelina ran up to Janelle and screeched, "Oh Janelle, I've missed you!!" Startled, Janelle responded, "Oh you remember me?" "Of course," Angelina replied... "You took me to the mall, shopping, to the movies and out to the restaurants to eat. Oh, I miss you Janelle." This was followed by a series of hugs. Janelle said she could see the love in this little girl's eyes as she remembered all of the good times the two of them had shared together. The children's grandmother, rather coolly addressed Janelle and, when asked, responded the children were fine, their mother was working, she was babysitting, and everything was o.k."

This grandmother, out of great concern, was the one who turned her daughter in to the DCFS in the first place. She was now guarding her words very carefully. She did not want to risk saying anything that would again jeopardize her daughter's custody of her children.

Our worst fear is concerning Angelina's being returned to a home where there are two unsupervised, possible sex offenders in the home. I cannot bear to think perhaps, once again, she has retreated to sleeping under her bed, or in a closet, in an attempt to fend off those who would abuse her. Our other fear is Armando, who at age nine had reportedly already joined a gang, may have recruited little Jose' into the gang lifestyle. Without counseling or supervision, and with his unbridled anger, the possibilities of what might happen to Jose' are overwhelming. We can only hope and pray that deep down in the resources of his soul Jose' would remember the lessons he learned while in our home environment, those of love, caring, non-violence, and that he is a worthwhile individual with tremendous potential. But, would these memories be enough to carry him through the rough teenage years? (One can only speculate...and hope. Our prayers are with you, our dear little angels, Jose' and Angelina. Vaya con Dios!)

Jimmy

"What do you get if you cross the Rain Man and Forrest Gump?" my niece asked us, as we sat relaxing following our Thanksgiving family gathering. "I don't know" I replied, "What do you get?" You get "Jimmy". We all burst with laughter. It was so true. It would be sad too until you get to know our little Jimmy.

The first time I saw Jimmy was at another foster home. He was sitting right in front of the TV with his nose practically touching the screen. He was watching Winnie the Pooh and rocking back and forth, front to back. Coaxed by his foster mother he got up and limped over to us. It was plain to see this little boy had a brace on his left leg and his left arm was smaller than his opposing arm with his little hand curled under. He came right up to me, tilted his head slightly to an angle and greeted me with, "Hi, I'm Jimmy Marshall. I'm pleased to meet you. Are you going to be my new foster mother?" I was taken back a bit because of his direct communication. From the information I received regarding Jimmy, he was mildly retarded, autistic, legally blind and had cerebral palsy. This little boy had suffered a stoke in utero, most likely due to his mother's drug and alcohol abuse, and had been born with three strikes against him. He was also premature and weighed in at less than four pounds. Somehow he survived, and after spending almost his whole life in the foster care system he was once again being moved to a new foster home. It is one thing to be born into this world with several developmental and mental challenges, but the thought of an innocent child beginning life with all these challenges, and then having been abandoned at the same time is almost unthinkable. My heart immediately went out to Jimmy and after a short visit I agreed to come and see him again. I wanted Jay to meet Jimmy so he would be aware of the tremendous task ahead of us before I gave our final answer. Jay met Jimmy the next day and he too felt as though this boy was to be the newest member of our family. We agreed and Jimmy was moved to our house the very next day. The foster family seemed anxious to have him moved as quickly as possible.

More than twenty-five years had passed since we took in our first foster child. Twenty-five years of progress, major changes in technology, we now have cell phones, computers, and the Internet. It is amazing to see the changes in our lifestyles brought on by the computer age. But one thing has not changed…those horrible black plastic garbage bags. They have now been enhanced with a pull string to secure them. But they still show up on doorsteps with little children attached to them. That was just how Jimmy arrived at our house…with two large garbage bags. One bag held his clothing and another held a variety of collected stuffed toys. Jimmy loves stuffed animals. He gets them for every occasion and he loves every one of them…and especially the ones that are blue.

New challenges came with this little boy. He was the first child in our home with multiple disabilities and physical limitations. Jimmy has been diagnosed with autism, mild retardation, legal blindness, left sided hemi paresis and he is shunt dependent. We are amazed, however, to see how well he functions considering his physical problems. He soon learned his way around the house and one would not notice his very limited vision…The most overwhelming adjustments with Jimmy living in the house though are the questions…questions…and more questions. Jimmy never stops asking questions. I have described it as the little voice we all have in our heads that holds conversations we do not verbalize…Well, Jimmy verbalizes everything. Some things make complete sense and are actually rather intelligent observations and reasoning, while other comments he makes just do not compute.

An obsession with relationships also elicits conversation. Jimmy needs to know everyone's relationship to everyone else in the room.

He'll walk up to each individual and very politely say "Excuse me, are you married?" "Do you have a wife?" Often at church he will approach people and ask the same question. In one case a young man replied, "No, I'm not married" to which Jimmy became very upset and started repeating, "But you have to be married, everyone has to be married, you must have a wife." It doesn't take individuals very long to realize this little boy is mentally challenged. Most people are very kind and just answer his questions. However, we try to be quick to intervene to remove Jimmy from the situation before he continues his barrage of questions that ultimately make people feel uncomfortable.

Incontinence is a problem many foster children share. Jimmy was no exception. We quickly realized without a "pull-up" for nights he would wake up soaked. We surmised also somewhere he had been punished for getting out of bed because no matter how many times we told him when he felt the urge to use the bathroom, to do so, he would not get out of bed to use the bathroom. He seemed confused and would say, "You mean I should get up and go use the bathroom?" "But I'm not supposed to get out of bed so early." We decided he had enough other issues to deal with in moving to a new home that being concerned with wetting the bed should not be one of them. We purchased a year's supply of child size "Huggies" and he would put one on at night and empty it in the trash in morning. This took some pressure off of this already stressed out little boy. Jimmy wore Huggies for about a year-and a-half. It wasn't until we had another foster child in our home with the same problem who was able to overcome it that Jimmy was able to follow suit.

Besides all of his physical disabilities, Jimmy also has some emotional issues to deal with. You see, not only was Jimmy born legally blind, with mild cerebral palsy and mild retardation, but to add to this, he was physically and mentally abused. My heart just breaks and then I get angry when I wonder how anyone could harm a disabled child. This is exactly what happened. When Jimmy was born and his mother saw his disabilities she decided she could not care for him so chose to give him up. Trying to be helpful a social worker talked her into taking him back. Unprepared and/or unwilling to care for him, Jimmy' mother neglected him. If that wasn't enough, one of his mother's boyfriends in a fit of rage because Jimmy was crying broke his leg. After this, Social Services removed him from his mother and brought him back into the State system. Jimmy's mother relinquished her parental rights and he has been a Ward of the State for almost 15 years. I wonder if this child may have suffered needlessly because of a social worker, though well intentioned, attempting to impose her wishes on the mother of this unwanted child.

Jimmy also has some food issues. He will not eat sweets, desserts, jello, pudding, ice cream....all of the things a child would usually enjoy. Another social worker explained to me these foods had been used in the sexual abuse of this tiny boy. To think of this makes me cringe. Finally after over a year of coaxing I said to him, "Jimmy, did someone do some bad things to you with food?" With head held low and in a whisper of a voice he replied "Uh huh". I then put the ice cream in front of him and said, "Jimmy, I'm so sorry someone did that to you, but you don't have to worry, no one here will ever do that to you. I want you to enjoy this because it is so good." He forced himself to try it and said he liked it; however, to this day if you ask him if he'd like some ice cream or dessert instinctively he will reply, "Oh, no thank you...."

It has been such an education learning about autism in children. I wouldn't have missed this learning experience for the world. Determined to help this child we began researching every avenue to inform ourselves about this unique and disabling disorder. A few quick facts that we learned about autism:

- Autism occurs in 1 in every 500 births and in a rate of 5 boys to every girl.
- Autism currently affects over 400,000 people in the U.S.
- Autism is the third most common developmental disability following mental retardation and cerebral palsy.
- Autism is more common than multiple sclerosis, cystic fibrosis or childhood cancer.

- Autism receives as little as 5% of the research funding as other less common diseases.
- The annual per-person allocation for persons with autism is approximately $35. In contrast, multiple sclerosis receives roughly $158, diabetes $424, breast cancer $600, and AIDS $1,000. Currently there is no medical cure for autism.

Some additional facts:

- Many kids are making enormous strides and a significant number are now indistinguishable from their peers.
- Behavioral therapies, diet, vitamin and mineral supplementation, and medical interventions are some of the treatments effectively being used.
- Most of the above interventions are considered experimental and are not supported by the medical community.
- Autism is a condition whose treatments are specifically excluded by some insurance companies.

What is Autism?

Autism is a biological disorder of the brain that impairs communication and social skills. It encompasses a broad spectrum of disorders that may range from mild to severe. Autistics have been described as being in their "own world." Many high functioning autistics describe two worlds; "Their world" and the "outside world." Many autistics describe their experience as "thinking in pictures," to quote Dr. Temple Grandin. There are serious sensory challenges that accompany autism, and some say are the source of autism, that must be understood to fully comprehend the disorder. Some of the markers are as follows:

Absence or delay of speech or language:

- Repetition of words in place of a normal verbal communication.
- Hand leading to communicate in place of verbal requests.
- Absence of verbal communication.

Difficulty relating to other children and adults"

- Absence of eye contact. (When directly in front of the child he may look in every direction, except at the individual in front of them)
- Apparent aloofness

- Lack of interest in other children and what the other children are doing.
- Lack of response to verbal requests.
- No response when name is called.
- Avoidance of physical contact (even with parents and siblings).
- Indifference to others in distress or pain.

Odd behaviors:
- Self-stimulation, spinning, rocking, hand flapping, etc.
- Inappropriate laughter or tantrums for no apparent reason
- Inappropriate attachment to objects

Obsessive compulsive behaviors i.e. lining up objects
- Repetitive odd play for extended periods of time. Example: stacking blocks for a half hour at a time
- Insistence on routine and sameness
- Difficulty dealing with interruption of routine schedule and change
- Possible self injurious behavior or aggressive behavior toward others

Sensory Challenges:
- Hyper (over) or Hypo (under) sensitivity of the five senses
- Abnormal responses to the senses
- A lack of response to pain or an overreaction to something seemingly minor such as a door closing.

As one writer so aptly put it "Imagine you were in a foreign, noisy and crowded city at night, not understanding the language spoken, recognizing a few words but not really comprehending situations taking place around you, wanting to express a need for help but not being able. This experience may begin to help you relate to what a child with autism feels on an ordinary day."

Autism takes on so many forms is can be very difficult to diagnose. In Jimmy's case, because he is so verbal, some doctors did not believe he was autistic. When seeking assistance from the local State agency for the mentally disabled, he underwent a series of interviews. Two psychologists at first did not think he was autistic. To convince them, so Jimmy would qualify for lifetime assistance, I decided to delay the interview until eventually Jimmy would get tired of talking with them. Then he would begin his display of autistic behaviors. First of all he would tell them "I'm through, and this is over." He then became agitated and began his "windshield wipers" which is a repetitive movement of his hands and arms back and forth across his chest imitating windshield wipers. Jimmy then started jumping up and down on one foot in a circle. This is called "stimming." It is actually a large muscle stimulation that calms the child down. Anyone with an autistic child knows you must have a place for the child to jump. When watching a TV show, Jimmy will get excited and start "flapping" his arms or he'll stand right up and begin jumping on one foot. The reason for the one foot is he has cerebral palsy with left sided paralysis so his one leg is smaller than the other and does not function very well. In the past two years Jimmy has undergone two surgeries to lengthen the tendons in this leg. Also the growth in his good leg has been stopped and surgery done on his paralyzed leg to lengthen it so both legs will be of equal length. He wears a brace and a lift on his shoe to correct the deficit.

Following Jimmy's display of autistic behaviors, the psychologist interviewing him said to me: "Well, I guess you are right, he definitely displays autistic behavior and tendencies." Jimmy qualified for the State assistance program.

Jimmy has been blessed with some wonderful physicians who have known him since he was a toddler and who sincerely care about him. I must mention Dr. Laurence McClish, an orthopedic surgeon who has operated on Jimmy at least twice. I recall one time when Jimmy was being evaluated for surgery on his short leg in anticipation of surgically lengthening the tendons. I took the opportunity to ask Dr. McClish if he would mind signing a letter I composed to send to the Shriners Hospital in California to see if I could get Jimmy on the list for treatment of his deformed hand. This could mean many trips over the mountain to Sacramento, waiting for appointments and being put on a list to be considered for corrective surgery. Dr. McClish said "Let me look at his hand." Jimmy willingly put out his little shrunken arm and hand for the Dr. to examine. Dr. McClish looked at me and said, "Oh, no problem, I'll just fix that while I am doing the surgery on his leg." You can imagine my astonishment and thankfulness to this wonderful doctor who had just saved me months of correspondence, waiting, traveling over the mountain and hoping to get on the list for treatment. In one swift, unselfish gesture he had made both Jimmy's life and mine so much easier. Dr. McLish also has clinics at the school Jimmy attends and children with a variety of orthopedic problems come to see him and are evaluated for treatment, including surgery, braces, etc.

I asked the doctor why he takes the time to do this when he has such a busy schedule. I was not surprised when he told me of his Christian faith and how he believes that God has so richly blessed him and now he in turn must bless others.

What a breath of fresh air was brought into our lives because of this dedicated physician.

Autism causes repetitive behaviors. Some of these help calm the child down, others help him to focus and others are soothing to him. These include everything from spinning, rocking back and forth, repeated hand movements, finger flicking, body slapping, and fascination with objects. Jimmy will come in our office and spin the chairs around or repeatedly open and shut cabinet doors or wiggle his fingers in repeated motions.

Jimmy has a fascination with windshield wipers. Every time we get in the car he asks for them to be turned on.... He doesn't always ask directly, but rather he will say something like "Is it raining today?" or "Don't you think the windows need cleaning."

He loves to watch their movements. Initially, riding in the car with Jimmy was somewhat of a challenge. He would become visibly upset whenever we would have to stop at a stoplight. He would start crying and say, "No, no, you can't stop, you need to keep the car going." Then the flapping movements would begin and he would start to cry.

It took months to overcome this. We found turning on the radio for him to listen to music helped calm him a little. I started explaining to him it was absolutely necessary for me to stop the car and he would have to deal with it. He would continue to mumble under his breath that "She just thinks she has to stop the car, but I know that the car should not stop, it is supposed to keep going"...and on and on. There were a couple of incidents when he got so upset that I just turned the car around and drove him home and informed him that until he could deal with the stops he would just have to remain at home. Jimmy worked very hard to overcome this obsession.

In order to fully understand autism, a thorough knowledge of the sensory challenges that autistics face is necessary. For a typical individual, we take the normal function of our five senses for granted:

1. Vision
2. Hearing
3. Touch
4. Taste
5. Smell

An example of the impact a dysfunctional sensory system may have is illustrated in *"A Walk in the Neighborhood."* A typical individual has no problem walking down the street with a friend, having a conversation, hearing the sounds of the neighborhood in the background, smelling the blooming spring flowers, and maybe chewing gum, all at the same time.

For an autistic individual, who has a dysfunctional sensory system, this typical experience may be completely overwhelming. The individual may be completely oblivious to the sounds of the neighborhood such as an ambulance screaming by, or may be totally overpowered by the smell of blooming flowers. The sun shining through the trees may be such an intense experience; it may inhibit the individual from being able to concentrate on walking down the sidewalk. Thus this inability to mesh the senses appropriately may profoundly impact someone's ability to "act" and communicate in a "normal" fashion.

Another obsessive behavior of Jimmy's is asking where we are going and how many stops we are going to make. One day I told him he could come with me as I went to the Post Office, the drug store and the grocery store. While we were out I remembered there were some clothes that needed to be picked up from the dry cleaners. I drove to the cleaners and Jimmy began questioning me about where I was going. I told him "to the cleaners." He immediately became visibly upset, crying and protesting, "You said you were only going three places and now you are going to four!!" I told him it was necessary to make the additional stop but I never heard the end of it, even an hour after we had returned home. He was still mumbling under his breath about the fourth stop and how unfair it was of me to say I was going three places and then to go four. Subsequently, we try to let him know ahead of time where we are going, but if it becomes necessary to make an additional stop, we tell him, "Jimmy, in the real world people have to make stops they hadn't planned on sometimes and you will just have to learn to deal with it." He used to be upset and annoyed but now, three years later, he has overcome that obsession.

We have had lengthy discussions about learning to be "flexible" and "accepting and learning new things" and he is doing his best. He often will remind us after he has tried a new food or gone to run errands with us which involve several stops, stating "I am doing pretty good at being flexible, don't you think so?" We encourage him with compliments as he continues to grow in this area.

Jimmy is an unusual autistic child because he is so verbal. We can enjoy a very normal conversation with him and he is slowly developing a sense of humor. His disability is so unusual in that one minute you can be discussing the affairs of the day, the weather, the news, family, upcoming events, on an adult level with him and the next minute he is back in his room playing with his "Bob the Builder" toys. These toys are targeted at an age level of about 2-5 years. He is truly a child-man and we must just accept the fact this is probably where he will always be.

We grew so attached to Jimmy and considered adoption so he could be reassured he would never have to go through the trauma of being moved again. However, this presented some unusual concerns. A good friend of mine, a social worker advised us against adopting Jimmy as his physical and mental needs are very costly and would pose an undo burden on our family. Recently the court did appoint us as Jimmy's legal guardian. This way he will not lose any of his benefits and he is content in knowing there is some permanency in his life.

We seem to learn a valuable lesson from each child who is placed in our home. Jimmy has taught us the love of God and a desire for a relationship with Him reaches even to the weakest and most challenged people in this world. Jimmy has an amazing faith in God, and a personal relationship with the Son. Jimmy's prayers are so beautiful and heartfelt. He loves to go to church and especially enjoys singing along with many of the songs he has memorized. Those he can't remember he will clap to the rhythm. It is a joy to observe him worship and give praise to God.

In the early years of foster care we were not supposed to bring religious teachings to the children. Thankfully that has changed and now foster children are given the right to practice their religion. It is my belief also that Social Services have recognized Christian homes have a very high success rate with foster children in their home. The children learn they are valuable and precious in the sight of the Lord.

Many Christian parents consider it a ministry of love to take in abused and abandoned children, to love them, and instill in them a deep abiding faith that will carry them through the rough times.

In one church service the pastor asked if anyone had made a profession of faith and would like to be baptized. Many people responded, including Jimmy. The pastor spoke with Jimmy and was thoroughly convinced Jimmy knew exactly what he was doing. Believe me there was not a dry eye in that church service when Jimmy, was hoisted into the baptistry by our pastor and Jay, and he stood on his one good leg, and tilted his head slightly as he quite often does in an attempt to focus his eyes.

After his profession of faith, Jimmy was asked if he would like to say anything. He realized he was the center of attention and that the entire congregation was looking at him. A huge grin came across his face and he excitedly exclaimed, "I feel I am very blessed to have a family and a church, and I am very happy to be baptized today." If this young man, with his many challenges, considers himself "blessed" how could any of the rest of us ever complain? The whole congregation broke out in applause for Jimmy's sweet testimony of his faith and happiness. "And a little child shall lead them."

Our research of autism has also shown us that there is hope! Autism is a spectrum disorder. On one side of the spectrum there are individuals who are mildly affected, who hold jobs and have families. There are PhD's and college graduates. There are most likely individuals you work or go to school with who are autistic and you don't even know it. On the other side there are severely affected individuals who require lifelong support, like our Jimmy. In between, there is a broad range of people. In addition, there are many famous people who have children who are autistic. The Miami Dolphin's quarterback Dan Marino, Buffalo Bills quarterback Doug Flutie, Former quarterback Jim Kelly, NHL hockey team Florida Panthers Captain Scott Mellanby, William Christopher of M*A*S*H fame, and Sylvester Stallone are just a few who are raising awareness and money for the cause. Today there are many more treatments and therapies available than there were ten years ago.

As it has taken over ten years for me to write this book, I can report that Jimmy's outcome is very positive. He is now 24 and works two hours a day at Job Training and Development at United Cerebral Palsy (UCP) Thrift Store and then has several hours of interacting with his peers through activities and outings. Having this job has been a godsend for Jimmy. He now has purpose and meaning in his life. He goes to his job with his head held high. He has had to learn to be flexible with schedules and work assignments. Being autistic, he prefers a rigid schedule and consistent job assignments. He happily gives us a daily report of his activities at UCP. He proudly announces to those he meets, "I have a job at UCP." His main job is preparing/cleaning used shoes for sale and placing them on shelves in the UCP Thrift Store. He is very conscientious about his job. We are so grateful to this organization for providing work opportunities for Jimmy and his peers. Jimmy has a bright outlook on life and is a blessing to all those who take time to get to know him.

Crystal

A year after Jimmy's arrival another child was placed in our home. She was eleven at the time of her placement with us. Crystal is similar to Jimmy in that she is legally blind, has mild cerebral palsy and is moderately retarded. Crystal is not as intelligent as Jimmy but what she lacks in this area she makes up in her physical ability and enthusiasm.

One thing about Crystal is she did NOT arrive at our house with the hated black garbage bag. Sadly, that is because Crystal arrived with only the clothes on her back and a pair of ill-fitting tennis shoes. That's right, not one toy, picture or additional piece of clothing. In addition, in the several years she has been with us Crystal has received from her relatives only one present at Christmas time three years ago, and not one visit. We understand her mother has been in and out jail for drug possession and her father died from suicide.

Crystal's mother did show up after a four-year absence. She contacted Social Services and asked for custody. Of course, she is fooling no one. She wants Crystal's welfare check to buy her drugs. Social Services is now seeking termination of the mother's rights because in the last four years she made no reasonable effort to complete a reunification plan.

Crystal has a leaking aorta valve and suffers migraine headaches. She is in special education at school and functions at a 4-5 year old level. She loves to help and sometimes gets into trouble forcing her help on others. This little girl has no stranger fear and absolutely no boundaries. She has now been with us four years and has shown some improvement in these areas.

We were informed by Crystal's cardiologist that she is diagnosed with Williams Syndrome. Having never heard of this syndrome, and wanting to know everything we could about it so we would know best how to deal with its symptoms, we did some research.

We found that Williams syndrome is a rare genetic condition (estimated to occur in 1/20,000 births), which causes medical and developmental problems.

Williams syndrome was first recognized as a distinct entity in 1961. It is present at birth, and affects males and females equally. It can occur in all ethnic groups and has been identified in countries throughout the world.

What are the common features of Williams syndrome?
- Characteristic facial appearance
- Heart and blood vessel problems
- Hypercalcemia (elevated blood calcium levels)
- Low birth-weight/low weight gain
- Feeding problems
- Irritability (colic during infancy)
- Dental abnormalities
- Kidney abnormalities
- Hernias
- Hyperacusis (sensitive hearing)
- Musculoskeletal problems
- Overly friendly (excessively social) personality
- Developmental delay, learning disabilities and attention deficit

Williams Syndrome, also known as Williams-Beuren Syndrome, is a rare genetic disorder characterized by growth delays before and after birth (prenatal and postnatal growth retardation), short stature, varying levels of mental deficiency, and distinctive facial abnormalities that typically become more pronounced with age. Characteristic facial features may include a round face, full cheeks, thick lips, a large mouth that is usually held open, and a broad nasal bridge with nostrils that flare forward. Affected individuals may also have unusually short eyelid folds, flared eyebrows, a small lower jaw, and prominent ears. Dental abnormalities may also be present including abnormally small, underdeveloped teeth with small, slender roots.

Williams Syndrome may also be associated with heart defects, abnormally increased levels of calcium in the blood during infancy, musculoskeletal defects, and/or other abnormalities. Cardiac defects may include obstruction of proper blood from the lower right chamber of the heart to the lungs or abnormal narrowing above the valve in the heart between the left ventricle and the main artery of the body.

Musculoskeletal abnormalities associated with Williams Syndrome may include depression of the breastbone, abnormal curvature of the spine, or an awkward gait. In addition, most affected individuals have mild to moderate mental retardation; poor visual-motor integration skills; a friendly, outgoing, talkative manner of speech and a short attention span with easy distractibility.

Following our research we now understand why Crystal looks like she does. She is a rather pretty, short in stature little girl, with an elfin look. She wears a size 7-8 in girls clothing and she is now 16. Crystal requires "line of sight" care because of her over friendliness and her lack of stranger fear.

To say Crystal has been quite a handful would be an understatement. She is very strong willed and physically strong, although she is only 50 inches tall she weighs 125 lbs. She is a very likeable, enjoyable girl, but if she gets in a tantrum mode she has been known to bite and kick. She may have developed these behaviors in order to defend herself...from what or from whom I do not know.

Another area of concern is the education provided for special needs children. I have been amazed at the systems that have been placed in special education to ensure these children reach their highest potential. Both of our children Crystal and Jonny were in special education classes. They are each received many services including physical therapy, occupational therapy, reading therapists, vision specialists, speech therapists, mobility instructors, personal aides in the classroom, and IEP's (Independent Educational Plans) to track their progress through the school system. At an IEP I once attended for Jimmy there were 9 people present including the school principal, special needs teachers, social workers, and even Jimmy's ophthalmologist. The government has certainly put in place regulations and requirements to ensure special needs children are educated in a manner equal to their peers.

I must say our children enjoyed a wonderful educational experience at school. Special Education teachers are very caring, well trained to meet their needs, and blessed with an unusual amount of patience. Jimmy integrated into several "regular" classes and also enjoyed field trips with his classmates.

Crystal loved school, and although her behavior was sometimes disruptive in the classroom, the teachers and aides assist her in her class work. Her senior year she worked in the office as an aide. She was so proud of the work she did there. On one occasion, however, Crystal decided she would make a copy of her hand and accidentally punched in 500 copies...fortunately this was noticed after only about a 100 copies had been made. She said she wanted to make a book.

Jimmy was given the task of filling the pop machines. He took this work very seriously and became visibly upset one time when the vendor did not show up with the pop and Jimmy could not do his job. In high school Jimmy's studies were geared more towards life skills and job training. He was very excited about entering this new phase in his education.

Crystal says when she gets older she is going to work at McDonald's. As she loves to help and clean things up, she just may be able to do that some day...with the appropriate supervision of course.

The Lunch Pail

One foster family, Bill and Lisa, went through the foster-to-adopt program and adopted a nine-year-old boy, Patrick, who is the younger brother of our adopted son, Brian.

Lisa shared with me that during her visitations with Patrick in his foster home, before he was placed with them on a foster-to-adopt basis, she met another little boy I'll call Adam. Adam had been in foster care for several years, and was in his current foster home for about 18 months. Lisa and Bill went to this home several times as "friends of the foster parents" so that they would have a chance to meet and get to know Patrick before officially applying to adopt him. Adam was quite excited about the prospective foster parents who were visiting his home, and I'm sure he was dreaming possibly when they visited, they might choose him to come live with them. However, this was not to be. Lisa and Bill had already decided Patrick would be the boy they believed the Lord had chosen for their family.

After several in-home visits, Lisa and Bill were allowed to take Patrick out on several outings so they could get to know each other better. On one such outing, Lisa took Patrick shopping and asked him what he would like to have. Patrick chose a shiny new lunch pail. Lisa thought this a little odd, thinking Patrick might have picked out a fancy toy, or electronic game, but Patrick was quite set on getting the new lunch pail.

When they returned to the foster home, Patrick couldn't wait to show off his shiny new lunchbox to the other foster children in the home. Lisa was so surprised when Adam, upon seeing the lunch pail, began to protest and cry openly, saying "It's not fair, Patrick gets a lunch pail." Lisa reached down to comfort Adam and asked him why he was so upset about Patrick's gift. "Because he gets a lunch pail, Adam cried… "And that means he's going to have a mom to pack his lunch." "It's my turn to be adopted, but Patrick is getting adopted first."

When Lisa shared this story with me, it just brought home again, how many little things we take for granted, but which are so enormous in the life of a child in foster care. The lunch pail, to this little boy, represented not just a present, but the whole concept of having a mother who would take the time to pack him a lunch for school.

This is something I am sure most children in regular families never even give a second thought…but to Adam, this was huge. Lisa also realized the importance of this too, and then it made sense to her why Patrick would select a lunch pail as opposed to a new toy or game. A lunch pail was so vitally important to him.

Through the years we have had many other children, just too many to include them all, but we remember them all…they are forever etched in our hearts. Each one brought something into our lives, and each one took a part of our hearts with them. We have such pleasant memories thinking of those sweet, cherub faces, those who came looking so forlorn and tired, some coming to stay with us for just a few days, some for months, and some for years.

I can picture little blonde curly haired Grant, just six years old, who came to us just before Christmas and stayed until the following February when his grandmother was granted custody of him. This was another example of a grandparent assuming the responsibility of raising a grandchild. Then there was Robby, an odd looking boy, so shy and awkward, but with the most loving and caring attitude. I don't really remember what became of Robby, other than that he was with us a few weeks and then he was gone. Then there was Richard who had run away from his foster home, as he just could not stand the stringent rules placed upon him in the home. We couldn't blame him. The woman running the foster home ran it more like an institution than a loving, warm home. She wore starched white uniforms like a nurse, a pressed white cap, and had her home organized like a military academy. We felt so bad about having to return Richard to that home, but ours was full at the time and there was no other suitable placement for him. He kept running away until he was placed in a juvenile detention facility. He had not broken any law nor done anything wrong, and yet this 12 year old ended up in a juvenile facility for juvenile offenders. This was such a sad commentary on the system at that time.

Brian

Since beginning the writing of this book one more little foster child has been added to our family. Our house is bursting at the seams. We are facing a new challenge.

The phone rang and a DCFS caseworker was on the line. "Mrs. Jeffers, I want to discuss with you the possibility of placing another child with you. I know your house is quite full, but this little boy needs just the environment you can provide." His name is Brian, he's eleven years old and he's been living at Kids' Kottage for over six months now and we'd really like to find a home for him."

Brian's story was like so many others. His parents are both drug addicts. Brian and his three siblings have been in and out of foster care for about 6 years. This last time the children had been picked up when their paternal aunt had called Social Services to report once again her brother and his common-law wife were on drugs and the children were not being cared for. The caseworker went out to investigate, and found the children, unsupervised, filthy, with ill-fitting clothes and shoes, and with no food in the house.

This same caseworker had removed the children once before from their home for the very same reasons. Social Services had provided the parents with drug counseling, parenting classes, and housing. The parents never followed up and the children had been placed with one of several aunts. However, this aunt also proved unsuitable to take care of the children. Investigation showed there were no suitable relatives available to take the children. The aunt who reported the neglect had already assumed responsibility for two other children in the family and was stretched beyond her resources.

I spoke with my husband, Jay, about the phone call from DCFS that evening. He arranged to go meet Brian the next day at Kids Kottage. I wanted him to make the decision this time whether we could take in one more child, or not.

Jay tells of his first encounter with Brian. The caseworker brought out this little boy, much too small for his eleven years. He stretched out his hand towards Jay and said, "Hi, my name is Brian, and I'm pleased to meet you." Jay's heart immediately went out to this little wisp of a boy, trying with all he had to impress this total stranger, who might remove him from his less than desirable living arrangements at the Kottage. Without much fanfare, Jay told the caseworker we would be happy to have Brian come and live with us.

Brian has done very well while in our home. He's had a lot to overcome. He had some inappropriate behavioral issues to overcome, and he was at least three years behind in his schoolwork. This would upset him at times and he would say, "I'm so angry that I'm so far behind just because my parents didn't send me to school because they were too strung out on their drugs." Brian attended Koinonia's school for children with behavioral problems and graduated after about a year. He began attending regular grade school and with the help of a special education teacher, and lots of help at home, he gradually caught up with his classmates.

Shortly before we adopted Brian, Lisa and Bill, with whom we have developed a precious friendship, adopted Brian's brother Patrick. Due to some behavioral issues the brothers could not be placed together. However, Lisa and I agreed these two boys would not be denied the closeness and friendship that two brothers should enjoy, so we arrange lots of play dates, and share special occasions such as birthdays, holidays, and vacations.

As he was the oldest of his siblings, Brian always felt responsible for them. It was not until the last one was adopted, and he was assured all of his brothers and sisters are well taken care of, that Brian could relax and begin to think of himself. Brian suffers from post traumatic stress syndrome due to the separation issues and the breakup of his biological family, but with counseling, and a safe and secure environment, he is making progress and is now able to relax and enjoy just being a twelve year old boy.

The parental rights of Brian's parents were terminated while Brian was living with us as a foster child. Jay had the unenviable task of telling Brian he would no longer be seeing his parents as their rights had been terminated. Looking through those big, blue, teary eyes of his, Brian replied, "That's okay because you'll adopt me won't you Dad?" Jay was lost for words, but said without hesitation "Yes, Brian, we'll adopt you."

Jay explained to me later, "I looked into the face of this adorable, blue eyed, blonde haired, fair skinned little boy with the Harry Potter glasses, and for just a moment I saw my own son." This little boy resembles our Brent when he was just eleven. "I can't help but relate. What if this was our Brent, begging for someone to adopt him, to take him in and love him, and become his parents. No child should be put in a position to have to "beg" for a decent home and security." Jay knew I would agree with him, and after much thought, prayer, professional advice, and soul searching, we decided this is what the Lord would have us to do.

Brian falls within the category of those children who most likely would not be adopted. He is over the age of 9, which for some reason seems to be the cutoff age for parents seeking to adopt. He had some personal issues, which for the most part have been resolved, with counseling, and the security of being in a permanent home.

At one time, when I was still in the consideration phase of the adoption, before making a final decision, I prayed and asked God, "Please, show me what we should do. We are in our 60's, slowing down, and living on retirement income. Please give me Your assurance and somehow let me know that this is Your will for Brian's and our lives." It was only about two weeks later when the Adoption Case Worker came to our home to see if we had reached a final decision on the adoption. I had quite a few questions for her that I needed answered. During our conversation she mentioned to me that, "As his adoption case worker, I am compelled to place Brian on the adoption Internet, as we must show the court we are making every effort to get him a permanent placement." Hearing that, something stirred within the depths of my soul. I heard myself saying to her, "NO, you are not going to place my little boy on the Internet, like a piece of goods for sale on EBay." Had I really just said that? I couldn't believe myself. But, yes, I had just called him MY little boy. This was it. This was the answer to my prayer. Deep in the reservoir of my soul I knew that God had given us this little boy to be our own, to love and care for. The decision had been made.

June 11, 2005 was National Adoption Day. Jay and I joined dozens of other families, in court, finalizing the adoption of our children. Patrick and his adoptive parents, Lisa and Bill were at court that day as "Ambassadors" for the adoption court.

Jay and I sat nervously awaiting our turn in the courtroom. Bill and Lisa were there, as were our adoption caseworker, and other officers of the court. This was a very special day. Brian was so cute, all dressed up in his suit and tie. The ceremony was formal, yet friendly and warm. The Judge was especially kind in her remarks and her appreciation to the families who had opened their hearts and homes to children in need. When it was finally our turn to speak, I could hardly say anything, I was so choked up. But I did manage to say what a privilege it was to welcome this fine young man into our home and family. I think I also said something about what a delight he was, and how courageous he had been through all he had been through.

It was Jay's turn to say something. His eyes welled up in tears, and he could hardly get the words out. He did share though how the very day he had picked Brian up from Kids Kottage, and Brian had asked him, a total stranger, on the way home, "Can I live with you forever?" Jay had responded at that time, "Maybe some day, Brian, we'll see." He then turned to Brian and said "Well, Brian, this is the day."

Jay, as a family counselor and licensed minister, does a lot of public speaking, and I had never seen him at a loss for words. However, this day, his emotion spoke much louder than words ever could have.

Bill and Lisa also were given a chance to say something. They were both so gracious, and I especially remember Bill's kind words about us and our family. He spoke of how he felt our family was the perfect place for Brian. Then Patrick asked if he could say something, and from his little 9-year-old heart, he told Brian how very happy he was for him that he, too, now had a permanent family. Patrick, along with Lisa and Bill, had been praying Brian would find a permanent home where he could be nurtured and loved. They knew their prayers had been answered.

Six months had passed since that memorable occasion. Brian was doing very well in our home. He still says things to negate his previous lifestyle and family. Quite often he would tell me "My old parents really didn't take good care of me. I'm so glad I have new parents." Or he would say things like, "My mother just wasn't a good mother, and I'm glad you're my mother now." Experience has taught me Brian is trying to sort things out for himself. Perhaps he even feels guilty at times for being happy and in a safe place. Lisa told me that one time Patrick said to them, "Mom I feel guilty because I love you guys so much." This is not uncommon for children to feel this way when they have been removed from their biological family, and placed in a safer, healthier and happier environment.

One day, after Brian had made some disparaging remarks about his mother, I said to him, "Brian, you do not have to hate your mother to love me. It's o.k. to love us both. You have a big heart and room enough to love two mothers. Your mother could not take care of you because of her drug addiction. She has an illness. We must pray for her that someday she will seek deliverance from her addiction." This seemed to alleviate some of the burden he was carrying for his mother. Brian rarely speaks of his father, except to say, "He was mean and lazy, and didn't take care of us." At that time, his biological father was incarcerated for battery on the children's mother, and drug possession.

Raising a pre-teen and then teenager did have its challenges, but there were also many rewards. I now do not have to wonder, or worry, what might have happened to Brian had we not adopted him. I know he is safe and secure with us. When I go in to tuck him in at night, and I see that angelic little face, sleeping soundly with a little smile on his face, I say, "Thank you Lord, for trusting us with this little life. Give us wisdom and strength to raise him into a fine, young man." Sometimes Brian will come into the kitchen, or living room, unprompted, and wrap his arms around me and say, "I love you, mom," and I know he means it.

At Jay's urging Brian joined the Navy ROTC in high school. Much to our delight, he loved it!! He enjoyed the structure and received straight "A's" in the class. Upon graduation Brian received an $80,000 Navy scholarship to use for continued education while in the Navy. He enlisted and is now a Seaman serving in Virginia. While so many foster children drop out of high school and then have difficulty finding a job or seek a career, the Navy was a wonderful choice for Brian. One month after graduation he left for boot camp, and is looking forward to a career in the Navy.

This is not exactly what we thought we would be doing in our mid 60's, and during our retirement years, but it is reassuring to know, as so often is said, that "God isn't finished with us yet." We are never too old to make a difference in this world.

As I was recording my thoughts to put in this book, I saw on the news where the State of Florida Foster Care System had "lost" a foster child, and could not account for almost one thousand other children in their system. This sounds outrageous, and it is, but one must truly understand the magnitude of the problems of foster care in the United States.

As of July 2013, 400,000 children currently are in foster care. 85% of these children are there because of their parents drug use. 85% of the parents will never be rehabilitated, thus the children will be left for society to raise, either in foster homes or through adoption.

Many of these children suffer physically, emotionally, and mentally from the effects of their parents drug use. Many children are born with fetal alcohol syndrome, suffer ADHD, (Attention Deficit Hyperactivity Disorder), require special education and medical intervention. Many social workers are overworked and underpaid and suffer "burn out."

Crystal has had 5 caseworkers in 3 years. The consistency we have enjoyed with caseworkers has been due to our children coming through Koinonia Foster Homes which contracts with the State to provide foster care. Through private agencies like this we are able to have close contact with the caseworker, immediate return of phone calls, continued support, and consistency of care for our therapeutic children. We are required to have, and receive, 20 hours of continued education each year. Koinonia also provides the format for this. There are also other agencies around the country like Koinonia and we would encourage anyone who is considering foster care to check with these private agencies.

We vowed to care for these special "chosen" children as long as the Lord allows and we have the strength and are able to do so. This has been our "passion" and "purpose" for over 30 years. It is both heartbreaking and rewarding. Someone has to do it and we feel privileged to be called to fulfill this place in the world.

Our hope for these children is that they will grow up feeling loved and accepted, find their place in society and live happy and productive lives. We believe every child deserves a happy childhood. We dream that someday garbage bags will only be used to haul garbage... not serve as containers for the contents of a little child's life. It will certainly be heaven on earth when there are no longer any "garbage bag kids" showing up on doorsteps with their tired little faces, worn out clothes, and those big, black plastic garbage bags.

Epilog

Returning home is not an option for approximately 126,000 children in the foster care system who were free for adoption in 2010. More than half of them are children of color. In 2010, 50,000 children were adopted from the public child welfare system—a 2% decrease from the 51,000 adopted in 2000.

Children and youth need opportunities to develop their talents and skills, to contribute to their families and communities, and to make positive connections to their cultures, traditions, and spiritual resources.

We prayed a suitable adoptive Christian home would be found for a delightful little boy named Brian. Several times over the years we have said, "All right, Lord, if no one steps up, we will adopt this child." Before Brian, the Lord had not required this of us and someone else had opened a heart and a home for a needy child. We trust in God's provision for "one of the least of these." This time God chose us. We will shower Brian with love and understanding, teach him about God's love and how Jesus said, "Suffer the little children to come unto Me, forbid them not, for of such is the kingdom of heaven." We are reminded that Jesus also declared "In as much as you have done it unto one of the least of these, my brethren, you have done it unto me."

On one occasion when I provided respite for a little girl while her foster mother kept some appointments, I overheard Brian saying to her, "Yeah, I used to be a foster kid, but I'm not anymore, cause I got

adopted. Maybe you'll be lucky too and someone will adopt you."
How wonderful if this would prove to be true.

This has been our journey through the foster care system. The
system is far from perfect, but it has come a long way from when we
began this journey over 30 years ago. It is not perfect, but it is the best
we have. What can make it better…more families willing to open their
hearts and homes and share whatever they have, great or small, with
the abused, neglected, abandoned, lonely, and lost children who live
within our community, and with whom we share the world.